VIEWPOINT

WORKBOOK 2B

MICHAEL MCCARTHY
JEANNE MCCARTEN
HELEN SANDIFORD

CAMBRIDGE
UNIVERSITY PRESS

CAMBRIDGE
UNIVERSITY PRESS

University Printing House, Cambridge CB2 8BS, United Kingdom

One Liberty Plaza, 20th Floor, New York, NY 10006, USA

477 Williamstown Road, Port Melbourne, VIC 3207, Australia

314–321, 3rd Floor, Plot 3, Splendor Forum, Jasola District Centre, New Delhi – 110025, India

103 Penang Road, #05-06/07, Visioncrest Commercial, Singapore 238467

Cambridge University Press is part of the University of Cambridge.

It furthers the University's mission by disseminating knowledge in the pursuit of education, learning and research at the highest international levels of excellence.

www.cambridge.org
Information on this title: www.cambridge.org/9781107572133

First published 2015

20 19 18 17 16 15 14 13 12 11 10 9 8 7

Printed in Poland by Opolgraf

A catalog record for this publication is available from the British Library.

ISBN 978-0-521-13189-6 Student's Book
ISBN 978-1-107-60154-3 Student's Book A
ISBN 978-1-107-60155-0 Student's Book B
ISBN 978-1-107-60631-9 Workbook
ISBN 978-1-107-57205-8 Workbook A
ISBN 978-1-107-60156-7 Teacher's Edition with Assessment Audio CD/CD-ROM
ISBN 978-1-107-66132-5 Class Audio CDs (4)
ISBN 978-1-107-67577-3 Presentation Plus
ISBN 978-1-107-56841-9 Student's Book with Updated Online Workbook
ISBN 978-1-107-56846-4 Student's Book with Updated Online Workbook A
ISBN 978-1-107-56849-5 Student's Book with Updated Online Workbook B
ISBN 978-1-107-56808-2 Student's Book with Online Course (includes Online Workbook)
ISBN 978-1-107-56809-9 Student's Book with Online Course (includes Online Workbook) A
ISBN 978-1-107-56810-5 Student's Book with Online Course (includes Online Workbook) B

Additional resources for this publication at www.cambridge.org/viewpoint

Contents

7 Relationships 50

8 History 58

9 Engineering wonders 66

10 Current events 74

11 Is it real? 82

12 Psychology 90

Units 7–12 Progress charts 100

Unit 7

Relationships

Lesson A Grammar Hypothesizing

A Rewrite the sentences with the underlined *if* clauses. Use the words or structures given.

STATIONS • ABOUT • SUPPORT • LOG IN • SIGN UP

PODCAST LISTEN LIVE SHARE

If you ask any parent about the challenges of a new baby, (imperative) [1] he or she will have stories to tell. My husband and I are no different. My husband was still in law school when we had our first child. If we had known (Had) [2] how difficult it would be to manage a new baby and school, we would have waited. My husband's classes were intense and our daughter was often sick the first few months, so we were both exhausted. If we did it again (Were) [3], we would be better prepared. At that time, I didn't know my new mother-in-law, who lived nearby, very well. If I had been (Had) [4] less shy, I might have asked her for help. One day, she happened to call when both the baby and I were sick. She came over in 10 minutes, told me to go to bed, and took care of the baby until I felt better. I was so grateful. After that, I asked her for help a lot. The lesson for new parents is this: Ask for help if you need it. If you don't (Otherwise) [5], those first months may be more difficult than necessary.

1. Ask any parent about the challenges of a new baby, and he or she will have stories to tell.
2. ______
3. ______
4. ______
5. ______

B Complete the sentences with the words in the box. One word is used twice.

Had	Otherwise	Should	Talk	Were

1. ______ I to start over as a parent, I would learn more about raising a child.
2. ______ I studied child development, I would have understood the different stages that children go through as they grow up.
3. My grandmother once told me, "______ you think raising children is easy, think again."
4. ______ to any parent and he or she will say that setting boundaries can be difficult.
5. ______ you decide to have a child, it is a good idea to read a book about parenting.
6. Take a class on what to do in a medical emergency. ______, you might not know how to react if something goes wrong.

About you

C Think about your experience learning English. Complete the statements with information that is true for you.

1. Had I known ______.
2. Were I ______.
3. Should you ______.
4. ______. Otherwise, ______.

Lesson B Vocabulary Expressions

A Complete the article with the expressions in the box.

above and beyond	sick and tired	stop and think	time and energy	wait and see
give-and-take	sooner or later	success or failure	ups and downs	

Living with roommates

Our college counselor describes some of the problems of living with roommates. She then offers solutions and advice for getting along.

If you __________[1] about it, living with roommates can be a big adjustment. In many cases, you will be living with people that you haven't met before. As a result, in the first few months you have to __________[2] how well you will get along. Even if you get along pretty well, __________[3] you are likely to have a few disagreements.

There will always be __________[4] when living with different people. Should problems come up between roommates, they can cause a strain on the relationship. For example, one roommate may complain that he or she is __________[5] of doing more of the chores. If one roommate believes he or she is going __________[6] what is expected, then there is likely to be resentment.

In order to have a harmonious relationship, there has to be __________[7]. You have to learn to compromise. Building a solid relationship requires work; you have to put in the __________[8]. Overall, the __________[9] of your relationship depends on each of you adapting to the other.

B Complete the sentences with a word from each box.

and	but	or	age	forth	suffering	think
			energy	later	surely	work

1. In this day __________, many people don't think they need more relationship advice.
2. If a couple has children, divorce can cause a lot of pain __________ for them.
3. My brother doesn't live __________ in the same city, so he has a long commute.
4. Sooner __________, most friendships change a little.
5. My grandmother was ill last year. Slowly __________, she is getting better.
6. If you are not sure what to do, it's a good idea to stop __________.
7. It takes a lot of time __________ to have a good relationship, but it's worth the effort.
8. It's hard having a long-distance relationship, traveling back __________ to see your partner.

About you

C Answer the questions with your own ideas and opinions.

1. Do you live with roommates or with your family? What issues do you face?

____

2. How are relationships different when you live with roommates instead of family?

____

3. What advice would you give someone who is having a problem living with a roommate?

____

Lesson B Grammar Information focus

A Rewrite the two sentences as one sentence. Keep the clauses in the same order.

1. Why do some couples have problems? It's usually obvious.
   Why some couples have problems is usually obvious.
2. What don't many couples understand? Daily communication is necessary.
   ____
3. It's important to agree on this. Where and when can you talk every day?
   ____
4. How do you resolve differences? It can be a big problem.
   ____
5. You should discuss this. How do you express your opinions kindly in an argument?
   ____
6. It's a good idea to decide this. How much free time do you want to spend together?
   ____
7. Should you tell your husband or wife this? Which of his or her hobbies don't you enjoy doing?
   ____
8. You should discuss this. How often do you want to go out separately with your own friends?
   ____
9. It's important to consider this. How much can you compromise in order to accommodate your partner's needs?
   ____

B Unscramble the sentences.

1. do / successful couples / is / What / talk about their problems
   ____.
2. the success or failure of your relationship / How / helps determine / you communicate
   ____.
3. can easily become / How many hours / a problem / you work in a week
   ____.
4. before you get married / whether or not / Discuss / you want to have children
   ____.
5. where / to live and work / Agree now on / you want
   ____.
6. is / their child might need independence / What / fail to understand / that / many parents
   ____.
7. approach problems in / children and parents / their relationship / How / makes a difference
   ____.

Lesson C Conversation strategies

A Complete the conversations. Write the letters a–e. There is one extra expression.

1. *A* My roommate is driving me crazy.
   B Oh no! What's he doing?
   A Well, ____
2. *A* I'm thinking about joining an online dating site, but I'm nervous about it.
   B Of course you are. It's only natural. I mean, ____
3. *A* Your family is so great. I just can't believe how well you all get along.
   B Well, we do argue, but we never stop speaking or anything, ____
4. *A* Do you think I should take a parenting class?
   B Yeah. Why not? I learned a lot from the one I took.
   A I'm just worried it'll take a lot of time. I don't have much free time.
   B Well, maybe you don't need to take a class. ____

a. in the end, you have to work things out.
b. In a word, she's great.
c. at the end of the day, most people are probably a little anxious at first.
d. When all's said and done, you can probably learn just as much from a book.
e. in a nutshell, he never cleans up.

B Choose the correct options to complete the conversations.

1. *A* My roommate and I really don't get along, so she's moved out.
   B Well, in that case, you'd better work it out. / You don't have to try to work it out, then, do you?
2. *A* My uncle is trying online dating. He's meeting a lot of interesting people.
   B So, in that case, it must be a good way to meet people. / So, he's not likely to meet anyone, then?
3. *A* Not a lot of online dates actually lead to lasting relationships.
   B Really? In that case, it's not ideal if you want to settle down. / It seems like people using online dating sites want long-term relationships, then.
4. *A* It's really hard to meet people. I never meet anyone new.
   B You shouldn't try online dating, then. / In that case, maybe you should try online dating.
5. *A* My best friend is really mad at me for some reason, but I don't know why.
   B You should talk to him, then. / In that case, he'll be really nice to you.

C Complete the conversation with the expressions in the box. Sometimes there is more than one answer.

at the end of the day	✓ in a word	in that case	then

Justina Guess what? I tried speed dating last weekend.
Samantha Really? How was it?
Justina Well, at first I felt really awkward. I mean, I'm pretty shy around new people. In a word,[1] it was hard.
Samantha So, did you meet anyone, ____________[2]?
Justina Yeah. I met a really nice guy. We're meeting for coffee Friday.
Samantha Well, ____________,[3] maybe I should try it.
Justina You should! ____________,[4] even though it was hard for me, it was worth it.
Samantha I think I'll try it, ____________.[5]

Lesson D **Reading** Family dinners

A Prepare Check (✓) the statements that you think are true about family dinners. Then read the article and check your answers.

1. They can increase children's language skills. _____
2. They do not affect the type of food people eat. _____
3. They may have a positive effect on behavior. _____

THE IMPORTANCE OF FAMILY DINNERS

1 In many of today's households, family dinners have become a thing of the past. With busy schedules held by both parents and children, many families rarely have time to eat dinner together. In recent years, nutrition professionals have been promoting family dinners as research demonstrates the benefits that eating together can provide to family members.

2 You may be wondering, "Why are family dinners so important?" Research has suggested that having dinner as a family on a regular basis has positive effects on the development of adolescents. Family dinners have been linked to a lower risk of obesity, substance abuse, eating disorders, and increased chance of graduating from high school. This document takes a closer look at some of these "dinner dynamics."

CONVERSATION

3 Conversations at the dinner table expand the vocabulary and reading ability of children. This benefit is not dependent on the socioeconomic status of a family; children in all families do better when they engage in dinner conversations. Dinner conversations allow children the opportunity to talk to their parents and siblings and to have an active voice within the family. They also provide opportunities for children to listen to others as well as express their own opinions. Family dinners allow every member of the family a chance to discuss his or her day and share any exciting news.

4 **Suggestions for conversation**

- Discuss the child's day. Ask questions that express your interest in your child's daily life.
- Discuss current events. Bring up news appropriate to the age of your child.
- Pick and choose. Create topics together; write them on a piece of paper and randomly choose one to discuss each night.
- Let all family members talk. Be an active listener and be sure your child learns to listen as well.
- Encourage your child to participate. Do not underestimate your child's ability to hold a conversation.

NUTRITIONAL QUALITY OF THE DIET

5 Eating dinner as a family has been shown to increase the intake of fruits and vegetables, which provide a variety of nutrients and dietary fiber. (For specific food group recommendations at various calorie intakes, visit the website www.mypyramid.gov.) Some studies also have shown that families who eat dinner together tend to eat fewer fried foods and drink less soda. Family meal frequency also is positively linked to the intake of protein, calcium, and some vitamins.

6 **Suggestions for mealtime**

- Make cooking a family activity and include everyone in the preparation process.
- Try fun recipes or old recipes with healthier alternatives.
- Have theme nights such as Italian night, Mexican night, or Caribbean night.
- Create your own original recipes using low-fat ingredients.
- Have family cook-offs.

DEVELOPMENT OF ASSETS

7 Internal assets such as having a positive outlook on personal future and a positive identity are linked to the frequency of family dinners. High-risk behaviors, such as smoking, are less frequent among families who eat meals together more frequently. Concerning boundaries and parental expectations, families who have regular family dinners are more likely to understand, acknowledge, and follow boundaries than those who do not eat dinner together. Self-esteem, motivation, and a decrease in high-risk behaviors are all related to the amount of time spent with family, especially during family dinners.

8 **Final family dinner suggestions**

- Have family dinners at least four to five times a week.
- Turn off TV, radio, MP3 players, and the like during dinner.
- Enjoy positive conversation during the meal.
- Spend at least an hour eating dinner, conversing, and cleaning up together.

SOURCE: University of Florida – Family, Youth, and Community Services

B Read for main ideas **Are the sentences true or false? Write T or F. Correct the false sentences.**

1. Despite people's busy schedules, families frequently eat together. _____
2. Nutrition professionals are encouraging more family dinners nowadays. _____
3. Research links family dinners to healthier weight. _____
4. According to the article, family dinners help children in math. _____
5. The benefits of family dinners depend on one's socioeconomic status. _____
6. Family dinners have been shown to affect the quantities of fruits and vegetables people eat. _____
7. Family dinners do not affect the amount of soda people drink. _____
8. Spending time at dinner with family improves a child's motivation and self-esteem. _____

C Check your understanding **Choose the correct options to complete the sentences. Write a, b, or c.**

1. Suggestions for conversation at family dinners include _____ .
   a. discussing the child's day
   b. discussing current events
   c. both a and b
2. A good way to promote productive conversations at the dinner table is to _____ .
   a. let one person run the conversation
   b. discuss the TV show that is playing while you eat
   c. think of topics ahead of time and then choose one
3. The author suggests that in terms of meal preparation, _____ .
   a. the whole family should prepare a meal together
   b. family members should take take turns preparing meals
   c. the children should prepare a meal for the adults
4. The author emphasizes that the food at family meals should be _____ .
   a. fun
   b. from different parts of the world
   c. healthy
5. Suggestions for successful family dinners include _____ .
   a. spending less than an hour on the meal
   b. turning off all electronics
   c. having family dinners at least twice a week

D Read for details **Complete the sentences with the correct word or phrase from the article.**

1. In modern times, families ______________ eat together. (para. 1)
2. Nutrition professionals have been ______________ family dinners. (para. 1)
3. Family dinners increase the chance that children will graduate from ______________. (para. 2)
4. Conversations during dinner give children an ______________ voice in the family. (para. 3)
5. Family meal frequency is linked to an increase in the ______________ of some vitamins. (para. 5)
6. ______________ behaviors are less frequent among families who eat meals together. (para. 7)

About you

E React **Answer the questions with your opinions.**

1. Are family dinners important in your culture? Why or why not?

   ____

   ____

2. How has modern life affected family dinners in your culture?

   ____

   ____

Writing Writing a magazine article

A Circle the best options to complete the sentences.

In the last two decades, technology has advanced in **a number of / a great deal of** ways we couldn't have imagined. We can now keep in touch with friends and relatives all around the globe with ease and often at **few / little** cost. By simply posting status updates and new photos online, **a few / a wide variety of** people – from our acquaintances to our closest friends – can receive immediate updates on our lives. One would think that such instantaneous communication would **lead to / effect** closer, stronger relationships. However, researchers have discovered that the growth in social media has resulted **in / to** greater isolation and loneliness for **a great deal of / many** people. For some people, simply having a lot of online friends has **little / few** effect on their sense of feeling connected to the people in their lives. As **a large amount of / several** researchers have noted, nothing can replace the power of face-to-face communication, which has **a range of / a large amount of** positive effects on our well-being.

B Complete the advice column with the expressions in the box.

creates	few	leads	number	result in	several

There are ________[1] strategies that can help people maintain a stable and lasting relationship. Simply following a ________[2] basic rules can allow your relationship to prosper. First, you should always be honest, as this ________[3] to a sense of trust, which is essential for all relationships. Next, it is necessary to be loyal. A ________[4] of people don't realize that sharing your friends' secrets or talking about them behind their backs can ________[5] serious problems. Finally, be sure to be generous in your friendship. Avoid selfishness, which ________[6] the impression that you only care about yourself.

C Editing Correct the error in each sentence.

1. There is a number of situations that can lead to tension in relationships.
2. It takes a great deal time to fully trust someone.
3. A wide range of factors effect how well roommates get along.
4. Most people agree that face-to-face communication leads greater satisfaction.
5. A large number of people is trying online dating these days.
6. It only takes a few effort to be a respectful roommate.
7. There is various ways that you can improve any relationship.
8. There are a number of factors that makes family dinners more enjoyable for everyone.

D Write a short magazine article in which you offer advice for the following situation. Check your work for errors.

My roommate is so noisy. She's constantly talking loudly on the phone, even when I'm trying to study. Then, when I'm just about to go to sleep, she turns on the TV. Sometimes she invites friends over late at night. I'm really frustrated. What should I do?

Listening extra Relationship troubles

A **Read the relationship problems that people might talk about on an advice radio show. Write two more possible problems.**

The caller . . .

☐ 1. has a difficult assistant.
☐ 2. has a boss who's unpredictable.
☐ 3. can't understand a professor.
☐ 4. wants to help a roommate.
☐ 5. has an annoying roommate.
☐ 6. has problems with a family member.
☐ 7. ______________________________
☐ 8. ______________________________

B **Listen to the radio show. Check (✔) the problems from Exercise A that are discussed.**

C **Listen again. Are the sentences true or false? Write T or F.**

1. Dr. Borgo has been practicing psychology for more than 25 years. _____
2. Sally's boss's mood is unpredictable. _____
3. Dr. Borgo advises Sally not to take her boss's criticism personally. _____
4. Dr. Borgo suggests that Sally get clear instructions from her boss about her work. _____
5. Dr. Borgo believes Sally's problem can be easily resolved. _____
6. Tarek's roommate has a habit of leaving his stuff around. _____
7. Tarek gives examples about his roommate with food, headphones, and a laptop. _____
8. Dr. Borgo advises Tarek to find another roommate. _____
9. Camilla wants more freedom and independence. _____
10. Dr. Borgo advises Camilla to call her mother a lot to resolve the issue. _____

D **Listen again. Complete the sentences with two words.**

1. Dr. Borgo says Sally should approach her situation ____________ ____________ .
2. He advises Sally to remain professional and positive regardless of her boss's ____________ ____________ .
3. When Tarek couldn't find his laptop he ____________ ____________ and called campus security.
4. Dr. Borgo advises that in his conversation with his roommate, Tarek shouldn't bring up ____________ ____________ .
5. Camilla's mother calls her about ____________ ____________ a day.
6. Camilla should tell her mother that she wants her in her life, but she needs ____________ ____________ .

About you

E **Give your opinion. Do you agree with the advice for each person? Do you think it will solve the problems? Why or why not?**

1. Sally: ____
____
2. Tarek: ____
____
3. Camilla: ____
____

Now complete the *Unit 7 Progress chart* on page 100.

Unit 8

History

Lesson A Grammar Referring to past time

A Complete the article. Use the verbs given and perfect infinitives. Some verbs are passive.

I _________[1] (would like / meet) Martin Luther King, Jr., the American clergyman and social activist. He _________[2] (widely acknowledge / advance) civil rights in American society through his program of nonviolent civil disobedience. A brilliant communicator, his famous anti-racism speech, "I have a dream," delivered on August 28, 1963, _________[3] (said / establish) him as one of the greatest orators in American history. In terms of concrete change, his main legacy _________[4] (consider / be) the passing of the Civil Rights Act of 1968, which prohibited racial discrimination in the U.S. His work _________[5] (also know / influence) the Black Consciousness Movement, which fought for civil rights in South Africa. His life certainly _________[6] (seem / have) an impact on the American people. Hundreds of streets have been named in his honor, and he will always be celebrated on the third Monday of January – Martin Luther King, Jr. Day.

B Rewrite the sentences so they make sense by adding a perfect infinitive.

1. Many human rights activists would like to discuss passive resistance with Mahatma Gandhi.

   ____

2. According to Nostradamus, the sixteenth century prophet, the world is supposed to come to an end on December 21st, 2012.

   ____

3. Sir Isaac Newton's 1687 work, "Mathematical Principles of Natural Philosophy" is said to lay the foundations for most of classical mechanics.

   ____

4. Jack Nicklaus is more than a great golfer – he happens to win 18 major championships.

   ____

5. As an art student, I would love to watch Leonardo da Vinci create one of his masterpieces.

   ____

6. Singapore statesman Lee Kuan Yew is acknowledged to help trigger the Asian economic miracle.

   ____

About you

C Answer the questions with your own opinions.

1. Imagine you were alive 200 years ago. Which famous figure would you like to have met? Why?

   ____

2. Who is acknowledged to have been an influential leader in your country? Why?

   ____

Lesson B **Vocabulary** Inventions that changed the world

A Replace the words in bold with words from the box with similar meanings.

apparent · gradual · lasting · profound · ✓significant · universal · visible

THE HISTORY BUFF

Vaccinations to stop the spread of disease have resulted in ~~**important**~~ significant[1] changes to our quality of life. Although the benefits are **slow to observe** ________[2] and not immediately **obvious** ________[3], vaccination campaigns have had a **deep** ________[4] and **ongoing** ________[5] impact on public health. Polio has become much less **conspicuous** ________[6], for example, and enhanced vaccination efforts could result in the **global** ________[7] eradication of many diseases.

B Circle the correct words to complete the article.

It used to be only the elite who could read, but the invention of the printing press in 1450 marked the beginning of mass communication and a **rapid / minor** increase in literacy rates. **Universal / Minute** access to new ideas undermined the entrenched authority of the church and caused **a major / an imperceptible** shift from religious to political power in Western Europe. The printing press also facilitated the **slight / massive** benefits of the scientific revolution, made possible by the sharing of information in scientific publishing.

C Complete the article with the words in the box that have similar meanings to the words given in parentheses.

immediate · insignificant · local · long-term · sudden · superficial · temporary

Compared to the sophisticated electronics in our homes, the humble plow may seem like an ________[1] (not important) invention. Yet the invention of the plow had a profound effect on humanity, and its impact was far from ________[2] (on the surface). An ________[3] (instant) benefit was that the process of growing food became easier and faster, and people could harvest more food than they needed. This led to a ________[4] (fast) change in human lifestyle. It freed up time for other activities, like trading ________[5] (from the area) products for other goods and services. These activities of storing and trading materials had profound, ________[6] (for a long time) benefits for civilization, driving – amongst other things – the invention of writing and number systems. While the plow was a ________[7] (not permanent) feature of history, its effects spread beyond agriculture.

About you

D Write about an invention that you think has had the greatest universal impact and why.

____

____

Lesson B **Grammar** Giving ideas extra focus

A Complete the cleft sentences using *it*, a correct form of *be*, and *who* or *that*. Some sentences are negative. Sometimes there is more than one possible answer.

This winter we will celebrate "On this day in history" by commemorating scientists who made significant discoveries.

FEBRUARY 19, 1473 On this day in history, Nicolas Copernicus was born.

________[1] Copernicus ________[2] educated the world about astronomy. ________[3] until his studies were published in 1543 ________[4] a centuries-old belief was dispelled. Copernicus demonstrated in mathematical terms why ________[5] the sun, and not Earth, ________[6] sits at the center of our solar system. This was a major discovery, and ________[7] his work in astronomy ________[8] is often cited as the beginning of modern science.

DECEMBER 25, 1642 On this day in history, Sir Isaac Newton was born.

________[1] thanks to Sir Isaac Newton ________[2] we understand the concept of gravity. ________[3] only when he explained its laws ________[4] we understood why objects fall down, and what draws them toward each other. While ________[5] gravity and the laws of motion ________[6] he is most famous for, his other discoveries are also significant. For example, ________[7] Newton ________[8] constructed the first reflecting telescope.

B Rewrite the sentences as cleft sentences with *it* + *be*. Add emphasis to the words or phrases that are underlined.

SEPTEMBER 22, 1791 On this day in history, Michael Faraday was born.

1. Electricity makes our lives easier <u>thanks to Michael Faraday</u>.
   ____
2. <u>His discovery</u> of using electricity and a magnet to rotate a wire led to the development of the electric motor.
   ____
3. <u>Faraday</u> became the first person to produce an electric current by moving a wire through a magnetic field.
   ____
4. Electricity became practical for use in technology <u>largely due to his efforts</u>.
   ____

About you

C Answer the questions about the three scientists and their discoveries with your own opinions.

1. Which of these scientists do you think is most notable? Why?
   ____
   ____
2. Which of these discoveries do you think had the greatest impact on our lives? Why?
   ____
   ____

Lesson C Conversation strategies

A Add the sentences in the box to the conversation. Then complete the expressions in bold to avoid talking about certain topics. Sometimes there is more than one possible answer.

That's always a big debate in our class.	I'm dreading my history class.
I can't believe how they just accept one view.	I feel like that, too.

Mike ________________[1] I know I'm going to argue about today's reading with this one guy in the class.

Kate Why's that? Do you have very different opinions?

Mike **Don't** ________________[2]! Let's just say that he has a really narrow outlook on life.

Kate I have people like that in my history class, too. ________________[3]. It's like they're afraid to consider other points of view.

Mike Yes, especially on things like foreign policy. ________________[4] . But anyway, **let's not** ________________[5]. It just frustrates me.

Kate Yeah, I know how you feel. ________________[6]. It's like people can't accept that sometimes our leaders got things wrong! But as you say, **that's a** ________________[7].

Mike Yeah, **I'd rather** ________________[8]. I have enough of that in my history class!

B Choose the most appropriate response to end each conversation. Write the letters a–d. There are two extra responses.

1. ***A*** I can't understand why so few students choose history as a subject. It's so important to our understanding of the world.
   B A lot of students think it's just about learning facts. But it's about much more than that.
   A _____

2. ***A*** Have you noticed how place names on a map often reflect a country's history?
   B Well, most places in my country have Anglo-Saxon or Celtic names.
   A _____

a. Exactly. That's what I'm saying. It shows that different cultures dominated at different times.
b. Right. That's what I'm saying. I don't accept that this is the most peaceful period in human history.
c. That's what I'm saying. It gives you a real insight into who we are and why we behave the way we do.
d. Yes, that's what I mean. I'm always wary of history that gives just one side of the story.

C Circle the best option to complete the conversation. Sometimes both are correct.

A If you look at history, wars often start because countries want what other countries have. You know, maybe a world government would solve that problem.

B Don't get me started / That's what I'm saying. There's no way it would work. Different cultures will always protect their interests.

A That's what I'm saying. / Let's not go there. Having no borders means there's no need to protect resources. They would belong to everyone.

B I just don't think it would work. I mean, imagine trying to elect just one world leader! Impossible. But that's another story. / That's what I mean.

A Well, I'd rather not talk about it. / That's what I'm saying. Let's talk about something else.

Lesson D Reading California Gold Rush

A Prepare Which of these statements about the California Gold Rush do you think are true? Check (✔) the statements.

1. ☐ The Gold Rush began in 1949.
2. ☐ Anybody who found gold during the Gold Rush period could keep it.
3. ☐ The Levi Strauss company began during the Gold Rush.
4. ☐ A third of all Gold Rush prospectors were dead within six months of arriving in California.

B Read for main ideas Read the article. Which of the statements in Exercise A are true?

GOING TO CALIFORNIA: 49ers and the Gold Rush

1 James Marshall found gold while working for John Sutter at his ranch in Northern California on January 24, 1848. He had been hired to build a mill for Sutter. This place would enter American lore as "Sutter's Mill." Word quickly spread through California, the rest of America, and eventually the world, and people flocked to California to make their fortune. Many of the gold seekers came from as far away as Latin America and China. In fact, according to some estimates, the population increased by 86,000 people in two years. Most of these treasure seekers left for California in 1849, hence our name for them: 49ers. Many of the 49ers themselves picked an appropriate name from Greek mythology: Argonauts. These Argonauts were in search of their own form of a golden fleece – wealth free for the taking. The trek was arduous for those who came over land. [1] ☐ It could sometimes take up to nine months to get to California. For the immigrants who came from across the ocean, San Francisco became the most popular port of call. In fact, San Francisco's population grew from about 800 in 1848 to over 50,000 in 1849. As a result of this growth, new towns, roads, schools, and churches were built.

2 The first lucky arrivals were able to find nuggets of gold in the streambeds. These people made quick fortunes. [2] ☐ It was a unique time in history where individuals with literally nothing to their name could become extremely wealthy. The gold was free for whoever was lucky enough to find it. It is no surprise that gold fever hit so heavily. Yet the majority of those who made the trek out West were not so lucky. The individuals who became the richest were in fact not these early miners, but were instead entrepreneurs who created businesses to support all of the prospectors. [3] ☐ It is easy to think of all the essentials this mass of humanity would need in order to live. Businesses sprang up to meet their needs. Some of these businesses are still around today, including Levi Strauss and Wells Fargo.

3 The individuals who made their way out West during the Gold Rush met with numerous hardships. After making the journey, they often found the work to be extremely hard with no guarantee of success. Further, the death rate was very high. [4] ☐ According to Steve Wiegard, staff writer for the *Sacramento Bee*, "one in every five miners who came to California in 1849 was dead within six months." Lawlessness and racism were rampant. However, the impact of the Gold Rush on American history cannot be overestimated.

4 The Gold Rush reinforced the idea of Manifest Destiny. America was destined to span from Atlantic to Pacific, and the accidental discovery of gold made California an even more essential part of the picture. [5] ☐ California was admitted as the 31st state in the union in 1850.

SOURCE: www.americanhistory.com

C Information flow **Find the correct places in the article for these sentences. Write the letters a–e in the boxes.**

a. Miners faced possible starvation or the contraction of a disease.
b. Known as the "Golden State," California represented a place where someone could start a new life and become rich.
c. Many made their journey on foot or by wagon.
d. Gold worth millions of dollars was found by a few miners.
e. For example, Samuel Brannan became one of the richest men by opening shops and selling newspapers.

D Read for main ideas **Are the sentences true or false, or is the information not given in the article? Write, T, F, or NG. Correct the false sentences.**

1. John Sutter found gold while working on James Marshall's ranch in Northern California. _____
2. James Marshall was obligated to share his gold with John Sutter. _____
3. The miners called themselves Argonauts after a group of adventurers from Greek mythology. _____
4. San Francisco's population grew rapidly during the Gold Rush because of all the new building there. _____
5. Early gold miners needed to acquire a license to dig for gold. _____
6. Most of the 49ers had no knowledge or experience of mining gold. _____
7. Only the lucky few who found big gold deposits became rich during the Gold Rush. _____
8. There was very little crime in the mines. _____
9. The miners generally worked 12 hours per day, 7 days a week. _____
10. The term Manifest Destiny refers to a belief that America would inevitably spread from the east side of the continent to the west. _____

E **Circle the correct options to complete the sentences.**

1. The gold miners were called 49ers because they _________ in 1949.
   a. set out for California   b. first found gold   c. arrived in California
2. The population in San Francisco grew to _________ in 1949.
   a. over 86,000   b. more than 50,000   c. around 800
3. The article describes this time as unique because it was the first time people _________ .
   a. became rich quickly   b. emigrated   c. found gold
4. The miners who went to the West all found _________ .
   a. gold   b. difficulties   c. jobs
5. The impact that the Gold Rush had on American history _________ .
   a. is often overestimated   b. was not significant   c. was enormous

About you

F React **Answer the questions with your own views.**

1. What did you find most interesting about the article?

____

____

2. What did you find surprising about the article?

____

____

3. Describe a major event in your country's history.

____

____

Writing Writing a narrative

A Circle the correct expressions to complete the narrative.

ABOUT US
INTERVIEWS
NARRATIVES
TIMELINES
CONTACT ME

Prior to World War II, my great-grandparents, Frank and Louise, married and were living in London. **As soon as / On** the war started, my great-grandmother discovered that she was pregnant, but, unfortunately, my great-grandfather was called to the war front six months later. My great-grandmother was **subsequent / subsequently** forced to evacuate London. Soon after **arrived / arriving** at her new residence, she had a baby girl. Sadly, three weeks later, she had news that my great-grandfather had been killed in the war. Deeply **saddened / sad** by this, she decided to give up the baby for adoption. **Once / On** the war ended, she returned to London where she had **previously / previous** lived with Frank and tried to find her daughter. However, in those days, it just wasn't possible. **Resigned / Resigning** to this, she married again and eventually had four more children – a girl and three boys. She died in 1992.

In the late 1990s, my grandmother was invited to be an audience member in a TV show. **Excited / Exciting** by the opportunity, she went along with her three brothers. They were amazed to discover that their half sister had contacted the show, **hoping / hoped** to find any siblings. **In the end / At the end**, all of my great-grandmother's children were reunited and the sisters became great friends.

B Rewrite the sentences with the words given and make any other necessary changes.

My great-grandfather left Italy for the United States in 1887.

1. He arrived at Ellis Island and then he was given a new last name. (on)
2. He settled in, then looked for a job and found one washing dishes in a restaurant. (once / eventually)
3. He bought a book to teach himself English when he had saved enough money. (as soon as)
4. He became the restaurant manager and that marked the beginning of a successful era for the restaurant. (after a while / participle clause)
5. He started his own restaurant, which my family still owns today. (in the end)

C Editing Correct the errors with *finally, at the end,* or *in the end.*

1. In the end of the war, my great-grandmother tried to find her daughter.
2. My great-aunt wanted to find her birth family, and thanks to the TV show, she at the end found her siblings.
3. At the end, the family members were reunited.
4. In the end of the TV show, the brothers and sisters exchanged contact details and promised never to lose touch.

D Interview a family member or friend. Write a narrative account of an interesting event in his or her life. Check your work for errors.

Listening extra The history of English

A How much do you know about the history of English? Check (✔) the statements that you think are true.

☐ 1. English has been developing for thousands of years.
☐ 2. French has been a major influence on English.
☐ 3. The Modern English era began in the nineteenth century.
☐ 4. There are three recognized varieties of English.
☐ 5. English has recently become resistant to change.

The gray countries show where English is spoken as the primary language.

B Listen to the podcast about the history of English. Which of the statements in Exercise A are correct?

C Listen again. Are the sentences true or false? Write T or F.

1. The early origins of English can be traced to Denmark and northern Germany. _____
2. About 20 percent of modern English words originate from Old English. _____
3. At one point, English was the language of the lower class in England. _____
4. The word *décor* was absorbed into English during the Modern English period. _____
5. We owe the standardization of English grammar and spelling to the Industrial Revolution. _____
6. The different varieties of English owe their existence to the British Empire. _____
7. Movies are one reason why American English is influential today. _____
8. These days, it's only technology that adds new words to English. _____
9. It's a fact that all languages are constantly evolving. _____
10. In the future, people might not understand the English we speak today. _____

D Listen again and complete the sentences with the missing words.

1. People from Denmark and northern Germany went to England _________ thousand years ago.
2. _________ years ago the French invaded England.
3. English became dominant again by the _________ century.
4. Modern English is divided into _________ time periods.
5. The Late Modern English period can be traced back to about the year _________ .

About you

E Answer the questions with your own ideas and opinions.

1. Have any of the words from your native language become commonly used in English?

____

____

2. How has your first language been affected by outside influences?

____

____

3. Are there different varieties of your first language, as there are with English? What are some differences between them?

____

____

Now complete the *Unit 8 Progress chart* on page 100.

Unit 9

Engineering wonders

Lesson A Grammar Unknown people and things

A Circle the correct words to complete the posting on a career advice website.

Job Profiles
Education Guide
search by state
search by field
Career Resources
Career planning
Relocating
Interviewing
Salary negotiating
Work at home
Retirement
Contact Us

CAREERS IN ENGINEERING

software_gal:

When I was a teenager, **whenever / however** I spent long hours at my computer, my friends would call me a "computer geek." I loved computers, so it was natural for me to major in software engineering in college. After graduating, I realized that there were jobs for software engineers everywhere, and I could move **whatever / wherever** I wanted to. I chose a company in Northern California because it gave me the freedom to work **wherever / whatever** I chose – from home, in the office, or even outdoors in the company garden! Furthermore, if no meetings are scheduled, I can begin work **whenever / whoever** I want and finish **however / whenever** late I want. As long as I put in 35 hours a week, I can follow **whatever / whenever** schedule suits me. I love my work and **whatever / whenever** a teenager with an interest in math and science asks me for career advice, I always mention computer science and software engineering. **Whoever / Whichever** said that it was boring to be a computer geek was wrong. Software engineering has turned out to be an exciting career for me.

B Complete the conversation with *-ever* words. Sometimes there is more than one answer.

A When I graduate, I'm going to study to be either a civil or an architectural engineer.

B Well, ____________[1] field you choose, there'll be a lot of job opportunities. I mean, ____________[2] you look these days – on the Internet, or company websites – you see ads for engineers. But engineering is kind of a difficult course of study.

A I know. But I'll do ____________[3] it takes to get into a good engineering program.

B Do you have a program in mind? Your grades are good, so I'm sure ____________[4] you decide to go for your degree, you'll get a good scholarship.

A Really? ____________[5] I ask about scholarships at school, they say they're hard to get.

B Well, ____________[6] told you that is wrong, especially in the field of engineering.

A That's good to know. Maybe with a scholarship I could afford to go to a really good school, and if I still need more money, I suppose I could work part-time.

B Well, ____________[7] you decide to pay for it all, I'm sure things will work out for you.

About you

C Answer the questions with your own opinions.

1. What field of engineering do you find the most interesting? Why?

____

____

2. Do you think it is worthwhile to pursue a career in engineering? Why or why not?

____

____

Lesson B Vocabulary Incredible feats

A Replace the words in bold with expressions from the box that have similar meanings.

ahead of schedule	constructed	erected	installed	positioned
assembled	delayed	✓ in a short time frame	maneuvered	

Incredible engineering projects

1. The Egyptian Pyramids of Giza, which are over 4,000 years old, were built **~~extremely quickly~~** in a short time frame, taking as few as 23 years from start to finish, according to some scholars. A big mystery is how the heavy stones were **skillfully moved** ______ into position by manual laborers, which was an incredible engineering feat.
2. The longest engineering project in history is the Great Wall of China, which was **built** ______ over a period of 2,000 years.
3. To avoid building directly on unstable permafrost, Chinese engineers raised the tracks of the Qinzang railway far above ground and sank the foundations deep into the mountain. Incredibly, this challenging project was never **stopped or slowed down** ______ . In fact, it was finished in 2006, three years **earlier than planned** ______ .
4. In 1885, the Statue of Liberty was transported from France as 300 copper sheets, which were then **put together** ______ in New York City. The sheets were hung on a metal frame that had been **raised** ______ on a large stone pedestal. The sculptor, Auguste Bartholdi, **carefully placed** ______ the torch in the statue's right hand. In 1909, an elevator was **put in place** ______ for tourists.

B Complete the paragraph with the words in the box. Sometimes more than one fits.

ahead of schedule	concrete	erected	in a short time frame	steel
completed on time	constructed	fell behind schedule	installed	

The world's tallest structures, 1889–1972

The Eiffel Tower was ______[1] between 1887 and 1889 to serve as an entrance to the 1889 World's Fair in Paris. At 300 meters (986 feet), it was the tallest structure in the world for 41 years, until the Chrysler Building was ______[2] in New York City in 1930. Towards the end of construction, the project ______[3]. Thus the tower was not open to the public until nine days after the start of the fair. In addition, although the elevators, had been put in place and ______[4] the work on them was not ______[5], so at first visitors had to ascend the tower by foot. It nevertheless was an incredible success, attracting almost two million visitors during the fair.

When the Chrysler Building opened, it was 319 meters (1,046 feet) high, but it held the record for height for only one year. In 1931, the Empire State Building was finished, and at 381 meters (1,250 feet) it remained the world's tallest structure for 41 years, until 1972. The innovative construction process included erecting a ______[6] frame that was then covered with ______[7] to make it stronger and to protect against fire. It was built ______[8] taking only 1 year and 45 days. The original plan was to construct it in 18 months, so it was actually completed ______[9].

Lesson B Grammar Emphasizing ideas

A Circle the correct options to complete the paragraph.

BUILDING THE
BURJ KHALIFA,
THE TALLEST
BUILDING
IN THE WORLD

In 2004, when engineers began to build Burj Khalifa in Dubai, **they had / did they have** many obstacles to overcome. Never before **they had / had they** attempted to build a structure 829 meters (2,722 feet) high. In the previous 30 years, **engineers had / had engineers** constructed only five skyscrapers over 400 meters high, and the tallest of these, Taipei 101, was only 509 meters. Furthermore, **the site posed / did the site pose** several challenges. Not only **the soil was / was the soil** on the site somewhat unstable, there were also intense winds. For these reasons **the foundation was / was the foundation** carefully designed to distribute the weight of the 163-story building broadly over the site. In addition, **a Y-shaped floor plan was devised / was devised a Y-shaped floor plan** to withstand the extremely high winds. Only after conducting 40 wind tunnel tests **the engineers felt / did the engineers feel** confident that the structure could withstand major weather events. The floor plan had an additional benefit – not only **it solved / did it solve** the wind problem, it also maximized tenants' views of the Persian Gulf. With complete confidence **the team began / did the team begin** construction in 2004, with plans to open the building in 2009. Little **they knew / did they know** that a global economic crisis in 2007 would delay the project. Fortunately, **the financial obstacles were / were the financial obstacles** overcome, and the building was opened to great fanfare in 2010. It now attracts businesses, tenants, and tourists from all over the world.

B Rewrite each sentence starting with the words provided.

Not every engineering project goes smoothly. The Central Artery / Tunnel Project in Boston, also known as the "Big Dig," was truly a feat of engineering, but construction was plagued with problems.

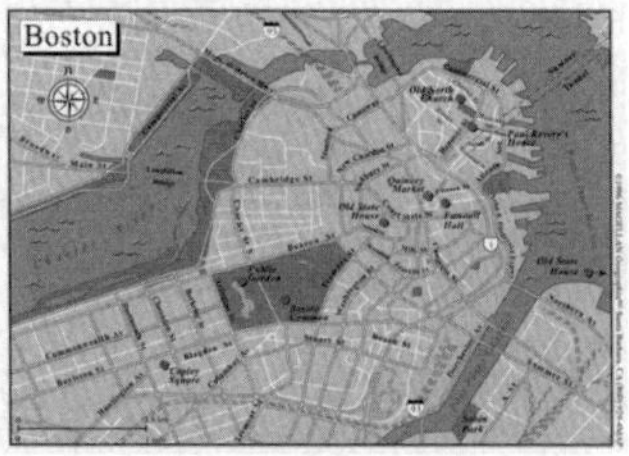

1. Such a large urban highway project had never been undertaken in the United States.
   Never before ______________________________________ .
2. When excavation began in 1991, the planners didn't know that the project wouldn't be done until 2007.
   When excavation began in 1991, little ______________________________________ .
3. They also didn't imagine that it would cost $18 billion more than projected.
   Nor ______________________________________ .
4. The project was over budget, and there were also many construction problems.
   Not only ______________________________________ .
5. Highway projects rarely have so many problems with the quality of materials and construction.
   Rarely ______________________________________ .
6. Some of the concrete was defective, and the tunnel light fixtures started to fall down.
   Not only ______________________________________ .
7. The lighting problem was solved by replacing all 2,500 light fixtures.
   Only by ______________________________________ .
8. The project is now complete, and the "Big Dig" is no longer the main topic of conversation in Boston.
   The project is now complete, and no longer ______________________________________ .

Lesson C Conversation strategies

A Circle the best options to complete the conversation. Sometimes both are correct.

Professor Today we're going to talk about engineering priorities for the twenty-first century. And the first thing I'd like to do is to get your opinions on what these priorities should be. . . .

Sun-hee Well, **given / in light of** our current energy needs, I would say that developing solar power is a major priority.

Pierre Right. But a bigger priority is to prepare for extreme weather, isn't it, especially **in light of the fact that / considering** what we know about rising sea levels?

Ana OK, but don't we need a comprehensive plan to address climate change, **in view of the fact that / considering that** we may not be able to keep ahead of the weather problems?

Somsak I agree. **Given that / In light of** all the predictions about the future, we have to do whatever we can to turn the weather situation around.

Ayshe You know, whenever the topic of priorities comes up, everyone talks about climate change, but what are we doing about clean water? I mean, **given that / in view of** 800 million people in the world today lack access to clean water, we can't ignore the problem.

Rashid No, but **in view of / considering the fact that** all the challenges we face, how can we prioritize? Shouldn't we try to address all the problems at the same time?

B Complete these comments with the expressions in the box. Then add *at all* or *whatsoever*.

no doubt	no effect	no interest	no need	no sense	nothing

1. We have ______________ for new highway projects. It just means more cars and more pollution.
2. It makes ______________ to build on the seacoast given all the flooding we've had.
3. Many companies seem to have ______________ in protecting the environment.
4. Some people do ______________ to conserve energy. They're just not concerned.
5. There seems to be ______________ that the climate is changing. Approximately 97 percent of climate experts agree on that.
6. People protest about pollution and environment problems, but it has ______________ .

C Complete the conversations with expressions in the box. More than one answer is possible and some expressions are used more than once.

at all	considering	given that	in light of	in view of the fact that	whatsoever

1. *A* It bothers me that some countries do nothing ______________ to address climate change.
   B Actually, I think most countries have taken some action, but ______________ the potential dangers, they obviously should do more.
2. *A* I hear that they're proposing to increase the number of nuclear plants, you know, ______________ nuclear power is supposedly cleaner than gas or oil.
   B You're kidding! I mean, ______________ all the nuclear accidents we've had recently, that doesn't make any sense to me ______________ .
3. *A* Sometimes I have my doubts about the safety of these new high-speed trains, ______________ there have been so many serious accidents lately.
   B Actually, I have no doubts about them ______________ . They're extremely safe compared to cars and buses.

Lesson D **Reading** Robots

A **Prepare** **What kinds of jobs do you think computers and robots will take over in the future? Check (✔) the boxes. Then read the article. Does the article present the same ideas?**

☐ barbershop ☐ call center ☐ clerical ☐ healthcare ☐ managerial

Robots are taking mid-level jobs, changing the economy

1 Computers and robots will replace humans in enough jobs that they will dramatically change the economy, said industry watchers and MIT economists at a robotics symposium Monday. And, they said, the transition has already started.

2 "What we're finally seeing is that our digital helpers aren't just catching up to us, but, in some cases, are passing us," said Andrew McAfee, an MIT economist and co-author of the book *Race Against the Machine*. "In some head-to-head contests, machines have raced past us."

3 Speaking at the symposium at MIT, McAfee noted that IBM's Watson supercomputer recently bested human champions on the *Jeopardy* game show. A Google self-driving car has been coursing around California, and the military is using robots on the ground and in the air in combat zones.

4 "We thought human beings held the high ground in a lot of these areas," McAfee said. "We looked around and suddenly saw computers doing things they weren't supposed to be good at. . . . We're going to see computers, robots doing a lot of jobs that humans are holding today."

5 But humans needn't get nervous.

6 McAfee isn't saying robots are about to become our managers. They're not going to run companies or hold department meetings. However, they will be replacing people in company call centers. They'll also be doing financial and industry analysis and a lot of mid-level kinds of jobs that people are paid to do today.

7 "There's a shift in how work gets done and how wealth is allocated," said Erik Brynjolfsson, director of the MIT Center for Digital Business. "Not so many people will be needed to work at H&R Block now that there's software to do our taxes."

8 Some jobs will be fairly safe at least for the foreseeable future, according to David Autor, an MIT

economist. Autor said that low-skilled and low-paying jobs, such as dog groomers, restaurant wait staff, and barbers, should be safe. Those are jobs that would be tough for computers or robots to take on.

9 High-skilled, high-paying jobs, such as high-technology workers and healthcare providers, should also be safe.

10 The shift is going to come in the middle of the workforce, Autor said. Mid-level paying jobs requiring mid-levels of education are in danger of being lost to technology.

11 "Think clerical and administrative support," he added. "Support and file and copy are more and more being done by machinery. . . . This is not unique to the United States, which makes it important as an [economic and global] phenomenon. In every country, middle jobs are contracting."

12 However, Autor said it's a fallacy that there's only a certain amount of work to be done and that machines will eliminate all jobs and leave people with nothing to do.

13 "Technology doesn't eliminate jobs altogether," he said. "And it does raise wealth. But it doesn't always have a positive distribution. . . . We shouldn't be worried that we're going to run out of jobs, but we may not like all the jobs being created. It's something we should be paying attention to."

B Paraphrase **The article presents six major ideas about technological change. Which ideas are presented in the paragraphs? Match the paragraphs and ideas. Write the letters a–e.**

a. Technology won't replace all jobs, but it may create some undesirable jobs.
b. Technological change is causing a global decrease in mid-level jobs.
c. Computers are increasingly doing jobs we thought only humans could do.
d. Computers and robots aren't replacing high- or low-skilled jobs, only mid-level jobs.

1. Paragraphs 2–4 _____
2. Paragraphs 5–9 _____
3. Paragraphs 10–11 _____
4. Paragraphs 12–13 _____

C Read for detail **Circle the correct options to complete the sentences.**

1. The robotics symposium heard that the use of computers and robots _____
   a. will not significantly influence the economy in the future.
   b. is already impacting the economy.
   c. has radically changed the economy already.
2. Computers are starting to do things that only humans were supposed to be able to do, such as _____
   a. operate vehicles.
   b. initiate military conflict.
   c. host game shows.
3. One thing people predict computers won't be doing is _____
   a. answering customer service calls.
   b. managing companies.
   c. helping people calculate their taxes.
4. The jobs that are most in danger of being eliminated are now those that require _____
   a. advanced education and skills.
   b. a mid-level education.
   c. little schooling or training.
5. Some people who are likely to lose their jobs are _____
   a. software developers.
   b. doctors and nurses.
   c. clerical and administrative staff.
6. According to David Autor, technology affects the job market by _____
   a. getting rid of jobs completely.
   b. generating less wealth.
   c. creating jobs we may not necessarily like.

About you

D React **Answer the questions with your own opinions.**

1. Which of the changes, if any, as described in the article do you see happening around you?

____

____

____

2. What do you see as the potential dangers of the increasing use of robots?

____

____

____

Writing A classification essay

A Complete the essay with the expressions in the box. Use capital letters if necessary.

another type	the first type	there are a number of
can be classified by	the second type	yet another type

Thanks to technological advances, ____________________[1] different types of robots. Robots ____________________[2] the types of jobs they perform. ____________________[3] is the rescue robot, which can save people in danger, such as after an earthquake. Clearly, they are useful for accessing places that are too dangerous for humans. ____________________[4] is the domestic robot, which carries out tasks around the house, like vacuuming. ____________________[5] is the mobile robot, which has the ability to move around as it performs tasks. These have started to replace workers in factories and are popular in the military. ____________________[6] of robot is used for medical purposes to assist with surgery and other medical procedures.

B Combine the sentences with the expressions given. Make any necessary changes.

The Palm Islands, in the United Arab Emirates, were artificially created by civil and marine engineers.

1. When creating the islands, the engineers used natural materials like rocks and sand. (as a substitute for) They did not use more traditional construction materials like concrete and steel.

   ____

   ____

2. To build the foundation of the islands, the marine engineers decided to use calcified rock from under the seabed. (instead of) They were going to use desert sand.

   ____

   ____

3. Engineers created 16 channels to allow water to circulate because they wanted clean, flowing water around the islands. (as opposed to) They didn't want stagnant water.

   ____

   ____

4. Because there was so little time in the schedule, the engineers made all their decisions on the job. (rather than) They did not research the project ahead of time.

   ____

   ____

C Editing Correct the error in each sentence. One sentence is correct.

1. Robots are better at some rescue efforts rather than humans.
2. It makes sense to send robots rather than humans into dangerous situations to save lives.
3. The military would rather prefer to use robots in many types of combat situations.
4. The police and the military use robots, as opposed for humans, to dismantle bombs.
5. "Virtual" robots are used as an alternative of humans to search the Web.
6. For certain tasks, people would rather have a human rather than a robot.
7. Most people would want a human server in a restaurant rather than to have a robot.
8. In many cases, robots simply cannot substitute to humans.

D Write a classification essay about different fields of engineering. Then check for errors.

Listening extra A student presentation

A Match the words and their definitions. Write the letters a–d.

1. the coast ____
2. a river delta ____
3. storm surge barriers, sea walls, dikes ____
4. an estuary ____

a. land where a river divides before flowing into a sea or ocean
b. where a river joins a sea or ocean
c. the land next to a sea or ocean
d. structures that protect the land from sea or ocean waves

B Listen to a student presentation about the Delta Works in the Netherlands. Then circle the best option to complete the sentences.

1. Over the past 1,000 years, the Netherlands has developed a vast system of dikes because ____ .
   a. 20 percent of its coast is on the North Sea
   b. the entire country is below sea level
   c. two-thirds of its land is at risk of flooding
2. The Delta Works was initiated as a reaction to ____ .
   a. an unusually devastating flood
   b. predictions of climate change
   c. a global interest in flood control
3. The Delta Works provides ____ protection for the people of the coastal area.
   a. the only
   b. extra
   c. little
4. Two of the sea barriers remain open except when ____ .
   a. the water is three meters above sea level
   b. the tide goes out
   c. the sea water comes in
5. The international reaction to the Delta Works project has been to ____ .
   a. learn from it
   b. ignore it
   c. criticize it

C Listen again and complete the facts and figures.

1. In the Netherlands, ________ of the land is below sea level.
2. In 1953, a storm surge caused the water to rise to ________ meters above sea level.
3. The Delta Works system will withstand the type of storm that only occurs once in every ________ years.
4. The Delta Works sea barriers protect ________ kilometers of dikes on the estuaries.
5. A planning commission estimates that the Netherlands may see a rise in the North Sea of ________ meters by 2100.
6. It is a fact that that ________ of the world's ________ largest cities are on flood plains.

About you

D Answer the questions with your own opinions.

1. What was the most interesting thing you learned about the Delta Works in the Netherlands?

   ____

2. Do you think other countries will invest in projects like the Delta Works? Why or why not?

   ____

Now complete the *Unit 9 Progress chart* on page 100.

Unit 10 Current events

Lesson A Vocabulary News analysis

A Complete the article with the correct forms of the verbs in the box. There are two extra verbs.

clear	compensate	escalate	make	mobilize	plan	plunge

TOP STORIES | NATIONAL | WORLD | BUSINESS | ENTERTAINMENT

Looking back at the challenges the president faced in his first term

The president certainly had his work cut out for him during his first 100 days. Just before he came into office, the stock market ____________[1] to a record low, resulting in job losses and economic stress for the country. The economy has since ____________[2] a modest recovery, but the country is still facing financial difficulties. The initial downturn prompted widespread protests against corrupt banking and corporate practices. The demonstrators were furious that banks refused to ____________[3] victims who had no control over how the banks handled their money. The president was actively involved in pushing for new legislation to mitigate these problems in the future. That did not stop the protests, however, and eventually authorities had to ____________[4] riot squads as tensions ____________[5] .

B Rewrite the bold parts of the sentences with expressions made up of words from each box. Write the verbs in the correct forms.

announce	cause	consider	contain	fuel	go	rule out	undergo

his campaign	off	speculation	the possibility
legal action	routine surgery	the explosion	the spill

Six months later, the president was faced with another challenge. A bomb **exploded** ____________[1] in front of two government offices, causing extensive loss of life. The investigation into who or what **was behind the blast** ____________[2] continues, and the president has not publicly **said it is not possible** ____________[3] that terrorists were behind the attack. Just as the nation emerged from that crisis, the country's worst ever oil spill occurred off the East Coast. It took weeks before the company responsible could **hold back the oil leaking** ____________[4], forcing the president to declare the area a national disaster. Damages have so far run into billions of dollars, and thousands of affected businesses are known to be **thinking about suing** ____________[5]. Finally, the president's sudden hospitalization a few months before the end of his term **encouraged people to wonder** ____________[6] that he would not run again. However, two days later, his press secretary confirmed that he was simply **having a simple operation** ____________[7], and a week later the president officially **said that he would run** ____________[8] his campaign for re-election.

Lesson A Grammar Reporting events in progress

A **Circle the best options to complete the news brief.**

NEWS BRIEF

An end to the fighting?

After months of bitter struggle, the tide now seems to **have been turning / be turning** in the civil war. Over the last few weeks, opposition forces appear to **have been regaining / be regaining** the ground they lost last winter. Furthermore, international peace brokers were said to **have been reaching / be reaching** a critical point in peace negotiations. Since arriving in New York on Sunday, representatives from all parties are said to **be negotiating / have been negotiating** a ceasefire agreement. Political analysts believe that prior to the talks, the president **may be holding out / may have been holding out** for outside military assistance, but he is now rumored to **be considering / have been considering** a power-sharing agreement with the opposition.

B **Complete the news brief with continuous infinitive forms of the verbs given.**

Possible student tuition increases

Thousands of students were said ______________[1] (prepare) for bad news ahead of an expected announcement of an increase in tuition fees. University officials and a representative board of students will ______________[2] (discuss) this divisive issue for two days by midnight tonight, which is the agreed deadline for an agreement. Despite some early signs of an agreement, hopes of reaching a compromise now appear ______________[3] (fade). Student leaders have warned that students would ______________[4] (take) action. Sara Folly, a political science major, had this to say: "I decided to skip classes and show my support to the board of students. The university authorities seem ______________[5] (not listen) to us. Free education is something I really believe in." Tensions in college towns are said ______________[6] (increase) since the start of the tuition discussions, and police are said ______________[7] (monitor) the situation closely.

C **Rewrite the underlined verbs. Add the verbs given and use continuous infinitive forms. Sometimes there is more than one possible answer.**

1. The president's health problems <u>are hindering</u> his re-election campaign. (say)

   ____

2. Hopes of a lasting peace <u>have grown</u> since the ceasefire agreement. (appear)

   ____

3. The public prosecutor <u>is considering</u> legal action against corrupt banking CEOs later this year. (think)

   ____

4. Sporting officials say that the games <u>have gone</u> smoothly so far. (seem)

   ____

About you

D **Write your own news report about a current event or situation that is causing concern.**

____

____

Lesson B **Grammar** Describing what should happen

A Read the journalism professor's comments. Then complete the textbook sentences that reflect those views. Use the subjunctive form of the bold verbs.

1. *"The mainstream news industry depends on journalism* ***maintaining*** *industry expectations."*
   It is important that the established press ____________ professional standards.
2. *"If certain editorial processes* ***are applied****, then quality journalism is possible."*
   It is essential that certain editorial processes ____________ to ensure quality journalism.
3. *First of all, a journalist needs* ***to consult*** *different sources to have sufficient background for a story."*
   It is crucial that the journalist ____________ various sources to establish the full context of a news item.
4. *Before submitting the story to the editor, he or she must* ***check*** *that all the facts are accurate."*
   Before the story is filed, it is essential that he or she ____________ all the facts carefully.
5. *You can lose readers if there* ***are*** *spelling and grammar mistakes, so any errors need to be* ***corrected*** *by a proofreader."*
   Readers demand that spelling and grammar ____________ correct. Therefore, it is essential that a proofreader ____________ errors before publication.
6. *"News providers lose business if stories* ***are published*** *late. Some have to show that they* ***are*** *the very first with breaking news."*
   It is necessary that stories ____________ as quickly as possible. There is a requirement on some organizations that they ____________ the first ones to publish breaking news.

B Circle the best options to complete the sentences.

1. Many viewers have said that a recent political documentary _____ accurate and objective.
   a. be b. was c. seem
2. To maintain press standards, it's crucial that any news item _____ completely error free.
   a. are b. reads c. be
3. The judge requested that the media _____ the victim's identity.
   a. not reveal b. not revealing c. not be revealed
4. The paper's insistence that the reporter _____ her sources was in line with reporting ethics.
   a. conceal b. concealing c. be concealed
5. It's possible for anyone _____ breaking news via smartphones and social media.
   a. be published b. publish c. to publish
6. Editors demand that their publication's reputation _____ by poor journalistic standards.
   a. be not harmed b. not be harmed c. are not harmed

About you

C Answer the questions with your own opinions.

1. Do you use a news source that you trust more than others? If so, what is it?
   ____
   ____
2. What makes some news sources more trustworthy than others?
   ____
   ____

Lesson C Conversation strategies

A Complete the conversation with the expressions in the box. Write the letters a–i. There are three extra expressions.

a. choosing your style	f. supermarkets, newsstands, even pharmacies
b. most tabloids	g. the content
c. my colleagues	h. the reporter
d. reading rumors and looking at celebrities	i. your choice
e. seeing them everywhere	

Zoe Have you noticed how many people read tabloids? Like, ________[1], they buy them all the time. I mean, ________[2], I don't know why they want to do that.

Chan-Sook I know. They're all about gossip and sensation. There seems to be a huge market for that kind of thing.

Zoe I know. And I mean, ________[3], they all sell them. You can't avoid them. It's so annoying, ________[4].

Chan-Sook Yeah, and, ________[5] of most of them, it's not really news, is it?

Zoe What gets me is all the bad news. I mean, ________[6], they're full of people's misfortunes.

Chan-Sook Yeah, well, bad news sells, I guess. You don't buy a tabloid newspaper to feel good about the world!

B Complete the conversation with *this, that, these,* or *those*.

A Hey. Did I tell you? There's ________[1] new tenant in my apartment block. And you won't believe who it is.
B Let me guess. It's one of ________[2] crazy celebrities from the tabloids.
A Good guess, but not quite. You know ________[3] anchor for the morning news on Channel 2?
B ________[4] handsome guy who wears bowties? Is it him?
A Uh-huh. We keep meeting on the stairs and having ________[5] really interesting conversations.
B That's amazing. He's smart. You know, how he asks ________[6] difficult questions in interviews.
A Yeah, and you know how he also has ________[7] quirky sense of humor on TV? Well, he does in real life, too. He's quite a character.

About you

C Complete the comments with information that is true for you. Then, explain your answer. Think of how to highlight the topics you are talking about. Try to use *this, these, that,* and *those* in your answers.

1. ________, they don't really appeal to me. I don't know why people watch that stuff. I mean,
____
____
____

2. It's ________, being able to get in-depth coverage of events at the click of a button.
On the other hand, ____
____
____

Lesson D Reading Newspapers

A Prepare **Why do you think the newspaper market has been declining? Check (✓) the reasons.**

1. ☐ The entertainment industry has become more popular than news. _____
2. ☐ Radio has taken part of the newspaper market. _____
3. ☐ The quality of journalism has declined. _____
4. ☐ People are reluctant to pay for news. _____

B Read for main ideas **Read the article. Does the author mention any of the reasons in Exercise A? Write Y (yes) or N (no).**

Why are newspapers dying?

The future of print journalism remains unclear

1 For people in the news business, it's hard to avoid the sense that newspapers are at death's door. Every day brings news of layoffs, bankruptcies, and closings in the print journalism industry.

2 But why are things so dire at the moment?

The decline begins with radio and TV

3 Newspapers have a history that dates back centuries. And while their roots are in the 1600s, newspapers thrived in the U.S. well into the twentieth century.

4 But with the advent of radio and later TV, newspaper circulation (the number of copies sold) began a gradual but steady decline. By the mid-twentieth century, people didn't have to rely on newspapers as their sole source of news. That was especially true of breaking news, which could be conveyed more quickly via broadcast media.

5 And as television newscasts became more sophisticated, TV became the dominant mass medium. This trend accelerated with the rise of CNN and 24-hour cable news networks.

Newspapers begin to disappear

6 Afternoon newspapers were the first casualties. People coming home from work began turning on the TV instead of opening a newspaper, and afternoon papers in the 1950s and 1960s saw circulations plunge and profits dry up. TV also increasingly captured more of the ad revenue that newspapers had relied on.

7 But even with TV grabbing more audience and ad dollars, newspapers managed to survive. Papers couldn't compete in terms of speed, but they could provide the in-depth news coverage that TV news never could.

8 So savvy editors retooled papers with this in mind. More stories were written with a feature-type approach that emphasized storytelling over breaking news, and papers were redesigned to be more visually appealing, with emphasis on clean layouts and graphic design.

The emergence of the Internet

9 But if TV represented a body blow to the newspaper industry, the World Wide Web may be the nail in the coffin. With the emergence of the Internet in the 1990s, vast amounts of information were suddenly free for the taking. Most newspapers, not wanting to be left behind, started websites in which they essentially gave away their most valuable commodity – their content – for free. This model continues to be predominant today.

10 Now, many analysts believe this was possibly a fatal mistake. Many once-loyal newspaper readers realized that if they could conveniently access news online for free, there was little reason to pay for a newspaper subscription.

The recession worsens print journalism's woes

11 Recent economic hard times have accelerated the problem. Revenue from print ads has plunged, and even online ad revenue, which publishers hoped would make up the difference, has slowed. And websites like Craigslist have eaten away at classified ad revenue.

12 "The online business model just won't support newspapers at the level Wall Street demands," says Chip Scanlan of The Poynter Institute, a journalism think tank. "Craigslist has decimated newspaper classifieds."

13 With profits plunging, newspaper publishers have responded with layoffs and cutbacks, but Scanlan worries this will make things worse.

14 "They're not helping themselves by whacking sections and laying people off," he says. "They're cutting the things that people look for in newspapers."

15 Indeed, that's the conundrum facing newspapers and their readers. All agree that newspapers still represent an unrivaled source of in-depth news, analysis, and opinion, and that if papers disappear, there will be nothing to take their place.

What the future holds

16 Opinions abound as to how newspapers can survive. Many say papers must charge for their web content in order to support print issues. Others say printed papers will soon go the way of the Studebaker* and that newspapers are destined to become online-only entities.

17 But what actually happens remains anybody's guess.

***Studebaker**—an automobile manufacturer in the United States that ultimately went out of business in the 1960s.

SOURCE: journalism.about.com

C Understanding viewpoints Check (✔) the points that the writer makes in the article.

- ☐ 1. The newspaper industry has always struggled in the U.S.
- ☐ 2. Twenty-four-hour cable news networks helped to make TV news dominate.
- ☐ 3. Afternoon papers were the first type of newspaper to disappear.
- ☐ 4. TV news tended to provide more in-depth coverage than newspapers.
- ☐ 5. Savvy editors launched new advertising and marketing campaigns to save their newspapers.
- ☐ 6. The decline in newspaper circulation began with the popularization of the Internet.
- ☐ 7. Profits from newspaper advertisements have been decreasing.
- ☐ 8. Laying off workers and making cutbacks is the only way forward if newspapers want to survive.
- ☐ 9. Other forms of media can't compete with newspapers when it comes to analysis and opinion.
- ☐ 10. There's a strong chance that free Internet content will bring about the end of print newspapers.

D Read for main ideas Circle the correct information to make true sentences about the article.

1. The history of newspapers began in the **seventeenth / twentieth** century.
2. In the middle of the twentieth century, sales of newspapers began to decrease **rapidly / slowly**.
3. To compete with TV, newspaper stories focused on **breaking news / detailed news coverage**.
4. Many experts think it was an error for newspapers to **go online and start websites / charge only for print**.
5. The conundrum facing newspapers today is that they are cutting back on what people **want / don't want** from them.
6. Some people believe that like the Studebaker, printed papers will become **a thing of the past / more expensive**.

E Read for detail Are the sentences true or false, or is the information not given? Write T, F, or NG. Correct the false sentences.

1. The newspaper industry has a long and largely prosperous history. _____
2. Newspaper workforces have lately been shrinking. _____
3. By 1950, TV advertising revenue had doubled. _____
4. To try and win back readers, newspapers changed the look of the page. _____
5. Most big newspapers have recently started charging subscriptions for online content. _____
6. Wall Street investors are hoping that online news will save the newspaper industry. _____
7. Craigslist is a more popular classified ads source than both print and online newspapers. _____
8. It is clear what the future holds for newspapers. _____

About you

F Imagine that you work as a consultant in the news industry. A news corporation has asked you for advice on how to encourage younger readers to buy their print newspaper. Write your advice.

____

____

____

____

Writing Writing a summary

A Read the summary of the article *Why are newspapers dying?* Circle the correct verbs.

According to the article, *Why are newspapers dying?*, the advent of TV and radio, amongst other things, **is / are** to blame for the decline of newspapers. By the mid-twentieth century, most people considered that breaking news **was / were** presented more efficiently by these new media, and this appealed to advertisers, resulting in a loss of revenue for newspapers. Since the rise of the Internet, free content **has / have** become the predominant online news model — a strategic error which unfortunately **has / have** lost newspapers millions in potential revenue. Finally, a number of recent developments **is / are** adding to newspapers' woes. Print and online newspaper classifieds **struggle / struggles** to compete with Craigslist, and the economic downturn of recent times **has / have** forced papers to cut content and lay people off. The author of the article **concludes / conclude** by wondering whether charging for online papers could subsidize the print versions or whether print papers will disappear completely.

B Complete the sentences with a correct form of the verbs given.

1. The revenue potential of the news websites ______________ not clearly understood when the Internet first emerged. (be)
2. In line with the trend at that time, online news ______________ provided free of charge. (be)
3. Today, the number of news providers with an Internet presence ______________ to include small, local papers. (grow)
4. People now ______________ to be able to download their news for free, and this has affected sales of print papers. (expect)
5. A number of newspapers now ______________ for online access, and readers who are used to free content ______________ to make a decision. (charge / need)
6. Quality reporting and free access ______________ available elsewhere. Therefore, do readers jump ship, or stay loyal to their original news provider? (be)

C Editing **Correct the sentences. There may be more than one error in each one.**

1. The number of blogs that analyzes the news have grown during the past five years.
2. The amount of spam that arrives in my inbox seem to be increasing.
3. The most exciting opportunities for someone who has been trained as a reporter is in online news.
4. The quality of news reporting that are available online are not always consistent.
5. The use of microblogs that is read by most young people have dramatically changed news reporting.
6. Satirical news and stories which appears on some websites are often believed to be true.

D Write a summary of an interesting news story. Be sure to follow the guidelines for summary writing. Then check your summary for errors.

Listening extra Journalism debate

A Read the expressions in the box, which are from a debate about journalism. What do they mean? Write the letters a–f.

1. a whistle blower _____
2. hack into (voicemail) _____
3. a code of ethics _____
4. a tabloid _____
5. a regulation _____
6. wrongdoing _____

a. behaving badly or illegally
b. an official rule
c. someone who reveals illegal activities in a workplace
d. a set of moral rules
e. a popular type of newspaper
f. access illegally

B What do you think the topic of the debate will be? Write an idea. Then listen and check your guess.

My guess ______________________ The topic is ______________________

C Listen again. Circle the best option to complete the sentences.

1. Dr. Gilmore thinks it is _____ for journalists to hack into email and other accounts.
   a. unethical b. unavoidable c. natural
2. He thinks that journalists need to _____ .
   a. be more careful b. regain public support c. regulate themselves
3. Marion McCall thinks the result of rules and regulations in journalism may mean _____ .
   a. greater social change b. better reporting c. wrongdoing won't be reported
4. She thinks unethical behavior by journalists is _____ .
   a. acceptable b. unprofessional c. widespread
5. Dr. Gilmore believes that the public has a right _____ .
   a. to privacy b. to newspaper records c. to see corruption exposed
6. Marion McCall believes that regulations should not prevent journalists from _____ .
   a. saving lives b. engaging in illegal activity c. making bad decisions

D Listen again. Complete the sentences with no more than four words.

1. We should be demanding that journalists ______________ email accounts.
2. Cases like the jailed journalists have had negative consequences for the ______________ .
3. Clearly, it's every journalist's responsibility to ______________ .
4. It's important that one consider the ______________ of a story, not just how it was researched.
5. A journalist might go into a social network or email account for information that ______________ .
6. There are always exceptional cases where journalists have to ______________ .

About you

E Answer the questions with your own opinions.

1. Which speaker did you think was more convincing? Why?

____

2. Which information presented in the debate would you like to know more about? Why?

____

3. Think of an example of an ethical dilemma that a journalist might face.

____

Now complete the *Unit 10 Progress chart* on page 101.

Unit 11

Is it real?

Lesson A Grammar Talking about the future

A Complete the blog post with correct forms of the *be to* expressions and the verbs given.

HOME
ABOUT ME
BLOG ARCHIVE
CONTACT

According to the weather report, another tropical cyclone ______________[1] (be / strike) the southern U.S. coast this week, severe floods ______________[2] (be about / hit) Western Europe, and the heat wave plaguing Australia ______________[3] (be set / continue). Perhaps, like me, you're wondering if all the damage and destruction from floods, tornadoes, and earthquakes ______________[4] (be set / occur) regularly across the globe. I did some research, and as far as I can tell, most experts attribute our changing weather patterns to global warming. Some of them say it ______________[5] (be bound / happen) sooner or later because our climate ______________[6] (be set / change) naturally every few million years. Perhaps that's true, but if the environmentalists are correct, climate change and natural disasters ______________[7] (be actually set / intensify) because of all the junk we put into the atmosphere. Hmm . . . so what kind of weird weather ______________[8] (be about / hit) your area? Personally, I think it's time to go green.

B Complete the sentences with correct forms of the *be to* expressions given.

1. If extraterrestrials exist, what would happen if they ________________ (be) turn their attention to our planet? Doomsayers regularly claim that aliens ________________ (be bound) invade Earth, and we humans will have to defend our planet!
2. How much importance can one attach to the sixteenth-century writings of Nostradamus? If you believe his followers, he predicted that France ________________ (be) undergo a revolution in the 1790s. Fortunately, his prediction that civilization ________________ (be) come to an end in 2012 has been proven wrong!
3. Some scientists say our grandchildren ________________ (be bound) experience severe food shortages if the population ________________ (be) continue growing at current rates. They estimate that humanity must shrink two-thirds by mid-century if we ________________ (be) avoid spiraling food prices and massive starvation.

About you

C Answer the questions with information that is true for you.

1. What events are about to happen in your city or town?

____

____

2. What is the weather in your area likely and not likely to do at this time of year?

____

____

3. What kinds of challenges are the people in your country bound to experience in the next few months?

____

____

Lesson B **Vocabulary** Idioms and phrasal verbs with *turn*

A **Match the words in bold with the expressions in the box that have a similar meaning. Write the letters a–f. There is one extra expression.**

a. turn a blind eye (to something)
b. turn down
c. turn out
d. turn (something) around
e. turn to
f. turning point

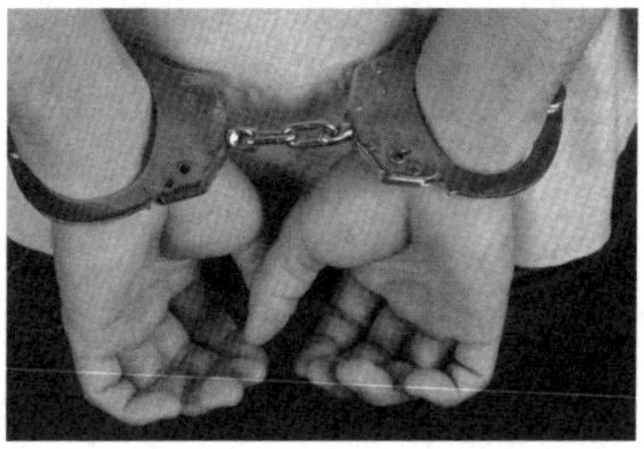

1. It's sometimes hard for people to **change** their lives **in a positive way** after they have gotten a criminal record. _____
2. There are some opportunities you have to **decline** in life. Not all of them are good. _____
3. Every person has a positive quality — sometimes you just have to **ignore** people's weaknesses. _____
4. Life can be difficult for young people if they don't have role models to **approach** for advice. _____
5. Most people can identify a **significant event** that really changed their lives. _____

B **Complete the conversation with correct forms of the *turn* expressions in the box.**

turn back the clock	turn out	turning point	turn (your) back on
turn into	turn over a new leaf	turn (something) around	

A You remember Jeff Kline, the big guy who used to frighten people in high school? He just called me to apologize, 20 years later!

B Jeff Kline? Wow, I can't believe it! So, has he ________________ [1] a nice person?

A Well, he was very apologetic. He said he knew he couldn't ________________ [2], but he wished he had behaved better all those years ago. And I know people who really like him now. They say he's ________________ [3].

B That couldn't have been easy — he had a difficult time when he was a kid. I remember he was always getting in trouble.

A Apparently, the ________________ [4] was when he met his wife. She helped him ________________ his ________________ [5] all of that.

B That's a nice story. And I'm glad things ________________ [6] OK for Jeff. You have to admire people who ________________ their lives ________________ [7].

About you

C **Use six of the *turn* expressions in the lesson to write sentences that have meaning for you.**

1. ____.
2. ____.
3. ____.
4. ____.
5. ____.
6. ____.

Lesson B Grammar Information focus

A Complete the blog post with passive or active forms of the verbs given.

Dreams • Thoughts • Ideas • Worries • Inspirations • Concerns

Home | About Me | Past Blogs | Contact Me

Are you someone who deserves ____________[1] (recognize) for staying true to your dreams? I'd like ____________[2] (place) in that category, but I've become more boring and conventional than I originally planned! For the last year or so, my mind appears ____________[3] (take over) by mortgage payments and other financial worries. Not only that, but life has gotten so busy and I can't avoid ____________[4] (catch up) in meetings and traffic jams. I have a friend, though, who seems ____________[5] (achieve) the life he always wanted. Nobody could ever ____________[6] (persuade) him that to a nine-to-five job was the way to go. No, sir! He'd rather ____________[7] (leave) alone in his beach cabin, to write, surf, and breathe in the fresh air. He says it's not worth ____________[8] (make) miserable by a regular job. He's just signed a lucrative book deal, and for that he really deserves ____________[9]. (respect) He's made it and he's avoided ____________[10] (force) to postpone the good life. How many people can say that?

B Rewrite the sentences using a passive form of the underlined verbs. Start with the words given. Sometimes there is more than one correct answer.

1. I want people to <u>remember</u> me for the charity work I do in the community.
   I'd like to be remembered for the charity work I do in the community.
2. My grandmother <u>taught</u> me to appreciate the funny side of life.
   I remember ______________________________.
3. My English teacher <u>has</u> unfairly <u>labeled</u> me the class clown.
   I don't think I deserve ______________________________.
4. I wouldn't <u>allow</u> sensitive viewers to watch a movie about me!
   Sensitive viewers shouldn't ______________________________.
5. My mother <u>gave</u> me all my sister's old clothes to wear, which I always hated.
   I didn't enjoy ______________________________.
6. I wouldn't want scriptwriters to <u>portray</u> my life dishonestly.
   I wouldn't want my life ______________________________.
7. My college <u>offered</u> me a graduate school scholarship.
   I didn't expect ______________________________.

About you

C Unscramble the questions. Then write answers that are true for you.

1. do you / What / be / to / appreciated for? / want / qualities
   Q: ____________________ A: ____________________
2. kind of career advice / given / What / be / today? / should / to young people
   Q: ____________________ A: ____________________
3. of your / you want / How / would / to be / life? / in a movie / portrayed
   Q: ____________________ A: ____________________

Lesson C Conversation strategies

A Complete the conversations with the expressions in the box.

be too happy about	doesn't sit right with me	that's not good
doesn't seem right	I'm not comfortable with	that would be my concern

1. *A* I have a friend who does a lot of online dating. But his profile isn't accurate. That just ____________________ to me.
   B Well, I think it's OK to emphasize the best parts of your personality, but ____________________ people who lie about things like their job or their age.
   A My friend wrote that he works in the theater, but he just has a cleaning job there. And his profile picture is about 10 years old!
   B If it were me, I wouldn't ____________________ that. I assume he's still looking.
   A Well, yeah, he is.

2. *A* My friend Sue asked me over to her new house, but I said I was busy again, which isn't actually true. I know ____________________, but I just couldn't face an hour in traffic.
   B It's too bad you don't see each other much now that she's moved. You'll end up losing touch. Well, ____________________.
   A Yeah. The problem is, neither of us likes driving in traffic.
   B Gosh. It ____________________ that something like that can get in the way of a good friendship.

B Rewrite the responses with *to me, to some people,* etc.

1. *A* You know what gets me? When people say they're going to get back to you about something, and they don't.
   B Yeah. ~~I think~~ To me that's rude, but some people think that's perfectly fine.

2. *A* I still haven't been paid for some work I did for a software company last month. Every time I call, they say my check's in the mail.
   B I don't think that's right. They probably think it's normal.

3. *A* One of my friends is always late. She calls to say she's on her way, but I know she isn't.
   B Yeah, no. What else does she lie about? I think that's also an issue.

About you

C Circle the correct options to complete the conversations. Sometimes both are correct. Then write your own responses to A giving your opinions.

1. *A* My friend asked me out on date, but I don't feel that way about him. I can't tell him that, though. **That's my concern / To me**, that would be too insensitive.
   B But if you don't say something, he might think you're interested. **That's my concern / To me**.

   ____

2. *A* My roommate gave me some of her stories to read, and they're terrible! I suppose I could tell her they're great, but **that doesn't seem right / I'm not comfortable with that**. I mean, she's hoping to be a writer one day.
   B No, **that doesn't sit right / that's not good**, either. **To me / I'm not happy about**, it seems like she needs some constructive criticism. I'm sure she'll appreciate that.

   ____

Lesson D Reading Second Mona Lisa

A Prepare The words in the box are from an article about a painting. Use the words to predict what the article is about. Write down your ideas.

art collector	earlier version	similarities and differences	the Mona Lisa
authenticity	Leonardo da Vinci	speculate	well-made copy

B Read for main ideas Read the article. Were any of your predictions about the article correct?

Second Mona Lisa unveiled for first time in 40 years

1 It's a mystery straight out of the *Da Vinci Code*. A famous portrait, hidden away in a Swiss bank vault for 40 years, with the potential to break open a mystery more than 500 years old. A second, earlier version of the *Mona Lisa* was unveiled to the public today, a version that experts say they can prove is the work of the master himself.

2 Known as the *Isleworth Mona Lisa*, the painting was discovered shortly before World War I by English art collector Hugh Blaker, who purchased it from the noble family to which it had previously belonged. Blaker then moved the painting to his studio in Isleworth, England, giving it its iconic name.

3 During WWI, the painting was moved to America for safekeeping. The portrait eventually made its way back to Europe, where it was analyzed in Italy before being sent to the Swiss bank vault for safekeeping. Since that time, experts from the non-profit Mona Lisa Foundation have been working to prove or disprove the portrait's authenticity.

4 "When we do a very elementary mathematical test, we have discovered that all of the elements of the two bodies – the two people, the two sitters – are in exactly the same place," art historian and foundation member Stanley Feldman told The Associated Press.

5 "It strikes us that in order for that to be so accurate, so meticulously exact, only the person who did one did the other. … It's an extraordinary revelation in itself, and we think it's valid."

6 Such similarities aside, the two *Mona Lisa*'s have many notable differences, the Isleworth version is larger and features columns on either side of the figure, believed to be Lisa del Giocondo. The version that hangs in Paris' Louvre Museum is narrower and features no such columns.

Isleworth Mona Lisa

7 The Isleworth painting was done on canvas, while the Louvre painting, which features a far more detailed background, was done on wood. The woman in the Isleworth version also appears younger than she does in the Louvre, leading to the theory that the portrait might have been painted earlier, consequently featuring a younger del Giocondo.

8 The foundation's claims aside, many in the art and scientific community remain unconvinced.

9 "It's a perfectly honest, well-made early copy," Martin Kemp, an Oxford University professor and da Vinci expert, told ABC News today. "Pictures were copied [because] you couldn't go to the Internet and order a reproduction. So if you wanted something like that [the *Mona Lisa*] and you couldn't get a hold of a Leonardo, you would order a copy."

10 With the debate still raging, it is difficult to reach a definite conclusion about the painting's authenticity. So, until the foundation releases more evidence, it looks as though experts will be left to speculate about whether the *Isleworth Mona Lisa* is the work of the Renaissance man himself, or one very gifted impressionist.

SOURCE: ABC News

C Read for detail **Are the sentences true or false, or is the information not given in the article? Write T, F, or NG. Correct the false sentences.**

1. A second, earlier version of the *Mona Lisa* was secretly kept in a Swiss bank for 40 years. _____
2. Hugh Blaker believed in the authenticity of the painting he bought. _____
3. The portrait was sent from Europe to America because at the time it was thought that America was a safer place. _____
4. During the twentieth century, the painting was kept in three different countries. _____
5. The fact that the women in the two paintings are in exactly the same position was discovered through a detailed scientific analysis. _____
6. The opinion of the Mona Lisa Foundation is that Leonardo da Vinci painted both versions of the *Mona Lisa*. _____
7. The total size of the two paintings is exactly the same. _____
8. Some people believe that the portraits feature the same woman painted at different times. _____
9. It's possible that Leonardo da Vinci made copies of his own and other people's paintings. _____
10. According to the article, in order to end the speculation about the *Isleworth Mona Lisa*, more experts need to analyze the evidence. _____

D Understanding reference **Find the sentences in the article. What do the underlined words refer to? Check the correct answer.**

1. It's a mystery straight out of the *Da Vinci Code*. (para. 1)
   a. determining who painted the second version of the *Mona Lisa*
   b. determining why the portrait was hidden in a Swiss bank vault
2. Since that time . . . (para. 3)
   a. WWI
   b. when the painting was sent to the Swiss bank vault
3. It strikes us . . . (para. 5)
   a. the people who work for the Mona Lisa Foundation
   b. the people who work for the Associated Press
4. . . . . in order for that to be so accurate . . . (para. 5)
   a. the fact that the two bodies are in the same place
   b. the fact that the parts of the two women are the same person.
5. . . . who did one did the other. (para. 5)
   a. the person who did the elementary mathematical test
   b. the painter of the *Mona Lisa* portraits
6. Such similarities aside (para. 6)
   a. the fact the sitters are in the same place
   b. the fact that the paintings are by the same artist.
7. . . . or one very gifted impressionist. (para. 10)
   a. an artist
   b. a fake painting

About you

E React **Answer the questions with information that is true for you.**

1. Which facts in the article surprised you? Which ones didn't?

____

____

2. What new things about art did you learn from the article?

____

____

Writing An opinion essay

A Circle the best expressions to complete the essay.

The case for regulating the rhino horn industry

Rhino horn has been used in traditional medicines to treat fever, rheumatism, and other ailments for thousands of years. Demand is at an all-time high, mostly supplied by illegal rhino poaching, and **given / no matter** what conservation measures are put in place, more wild rhinos are being killed each year. Some animal activists question why the industry exists at all, **considering that / provided that** rhino horn is composed entirely of keratin (the chief component in hair and fingernails). **In view of the fact / Yet** others point out that rhino horn is a cultural icon, and people have the right to use it **regardless of / in light of** skeptics who deny its medicinal effectiveness. Fortunately, there is a way to preserve rhinos and supply the horn market at the same time. Like hair and nails, rhino horn grows back, **as long as / yet** it isn't entirely removed. So it can be farmed in captive breeding programs, a practice that already exists in China. Therefore, **in view of the fact / no matter** that certain subspecies could soon become extinct, it is my opinion that governments should issue rhino-farming licenses and regulate the rhino-horn industry.

B Complete the sentences with the expressions in the box. Sometimes more than one answer is possible.

given that	in light of	irrespective of	provided	regardless of	yet

1. The killing of rhinos can be stopped ________________ the authorities are willing to regulate the rhino-horn market. The question is, will they?
2. The market for illegal products will continue to exist ________________ government attempts to prohibit such industries.
3. Demand for rhino horn is set to grow ________________ the recent rumor that powdered rhino horn can cure cancer.
4. Banning the trade in endangered species seems to push animals closer to extinction, ________________ how severe the penalties are.
5. Businesses are often efficient at producing and protecting valuable species. ________________ governments seem reluctant to involve them in conservation.
6. The trade in rhino horn should be legalized ________________ it is possible to remove most of the horn without harming the animal.

C Editing Correct the sentences by replacing the underlined expressions with other conjunctions or adverbs from the lesson. Sometimes more than one answer is possible.

1. Some people think that the rhino horn ban can work <u>provided that</u> the ivory ban worked. However, the long-term success of the ivory ban remains questionable.
2. The illegal trade of animal body parts continues <u>assuming</u> the fact that many animal species are close to extinction.
3. There is a thriving, legal trade in farmed crocodile skin that has not affected wild crocodiles. <u>As long as</u> some people think a legal trade in rhino horn would endanger wild rhinos.
4. Endangered species can be saved <u>given that</u> governments explore ways to protect them.

D Write an essay giving your opinion about the market for endangered animal products. Use the academic conjunctions and adverbs from this lesson. Then check your essay for errors.

Listening extra Fake résumés

A Look at the list of things that some people have been known to falsify on résumés and job applications. Write three more things.

JOHN SMITH

Philadelphia, Pennsylvania
(555) 555-5555
John_Smith@cup.com

OBJECTIVE:

Be a productive team leader that moves the company forward

PROFESSIONAL EXPERIENCE:

VP of International Sales for Acme Soda, Inc.	2012-Current
National Sales Manager for Philly Soda, Inc.	2000-2012
District Sales Manager for Philly Soda, Inc.	1998-2000
Salesman for Philly Soda, Inc.	1996-1998

EDUCATION:

- ☐ current job title
- ☐ current salary
- ☐ date of birth
- ☐ education
- ☐ periods of unemployment
- ☐ reason for leaving a job
- ☐ references
- ______________________
- ______________________
- ______________________

B Listen to the interview about false information on résumés. Check (✔) the items above that the people talk about.

C Listen again. Check (✔) the correct answers to the questions.

1. What are you likely to find on most résumés?
   - ☐ a. exaggerations
   - ☐ b. false job descriptions
2. How can managers prevent their companies from wasting time and money?
   - ☐ a. by not interviewing suspicious candidates
   - ☐ b. by doing phone interviews
3. What makes Sarah Lim become suspicious?
   - ☐ a. job descriptions that don't match skills and experience
   - ☐ b. unexplained periods of unemployment
4. What kind of fake education information do some candidates provide?
   - ☐ a. They claim to have attended prestigious schools.
   - ☐ b. They list degrees that they haven't actually completed.
5. What can suggest fake work experience?
   - ☐ a. candidates listing companies with technical names
   - ☐ b. candidates listing companies with unusual addresses
6. How does Sarah Lim check salary information?
   - ☐ a. She asks applicants to provide their last tax return.
   - ☐ b. She asks applicants to provide their last paycheck.
7. What warning does she give about references?
   - ☐ a. Some candidates list relatives as references.
   - ☐ b. Some candidates write their own references.

About you

D What do you think about putting false information on a résumé? Complete the sentences with your own views.

1. To me ____.
2. I'm not comfortable with ______________________________________.
3. ____. That would be my concern.

Now complete the *Unit 11 Progress chart* on page 101.

Unit 12 Psychology

Lesson A Grammar Complex situations and events

A **Put the words in bold into the correct order to complete the sentences in the email.**

I drove up to New York to visit my mom last weekend. I was kind of tired, but I knew **me / relaxing / to / wouldn't / she / kindly / take** ______________[1] in front of the TV. As I expected, **on / she / insisted / us / going** ______________[2] to see a Broadway show, followed by a meal at a fancy restaurant! It was fun, although **enjoy / didn't / driving / I / her** ______________[3] through several red lights on the way to the theater. I hadn't realized how much her eyesight had deteriorated, and I had to express **about / causing / my / concerns / her** ______________[4] a serious accident. It was quite a difficult moment, actually. **her / looking / I / remember** ______________[5] straight ahead and not saying anything. For the first time, **with / we / were / getting / her / dealing** ______________[6] old and the implications of that for the two of us.

B **Read the rest of the email. Rewrite the bold parts of the sentences with an object and an *-ing* form.**

I think the driving situation allowed my mom to talk candidly about things. She said she **didn't like the fact that I lived** didn't like me living[1] so far away. Also, she didn't trust accountants, and she wasn't **comfortable with the fact that they handled** ______________[2] her finances. She wanted us to live closer, and she wanted me to look after her accounts from now on. I guess this was bound to happen at some point, but it was still a shock. My mother's always been a big **believer in the idea that people should be** ______________[3] independent, and I **recall that she always said** ______________[4] that I should always think for myself. I hate to **insist that she should give up the car** ______________[5], but I guess we're moving onto a new stage in life, where I have to guide her.

About you

C **Complete the sentences to make them true for you. Use an *-ing* form and any other information.**

1. When I was growing up, I remember my mother ______________________________.
2. In my opinion, parents should always insist on their children ______________________________.
3. I'm a great believer in people ______________________________.

Lesson B **Vocabulary** Phrasal verbs

A Circle the correct phrasal verbs to complete the anecdote.

Beware of con artists on classified ad websites! I learned that last summer when I used the Internet to look for a new apartment. The price of the one I **picked out / picked up on** — a renovated loft — seemed very reasonable, if the upscale neighborhood was anything to **give away / go by**. However, that didn't strike me as suspicious and I rushed to put down a deposit. A few days later, the ad was still up, listing the apartment as "available." I really should have **talked into / picked up on** the scam at that point, but I **was taken in by / played down** the "agent's" explanation. He said he'd forgotten his password to the website so he couldn't take the ad down. What finally **gave the game away / went by** was someone arriving to view the apartment while I was measuring it for new furniture! Of course, by then the agent had disappeared with the deposits of several naive "tenants." I guess it **comes down to / went about** the old saying: If it seems too good to be true, it probably is!

B Complete each sentence with a verb (in the correct form) from box A and a word from box B.

A				
give	go	play	put	talk

B				
about	away	behind	down	into

1. My boyfriend started seeing someone else! What ________ him ________ was her photo in his wallet.
2. I'm always wary of people who try to ________ you ________ quick moneymaking schemes.
3. Dreaming up ways to scam people isn't the best way to ________ ________ earning a living.
4. If you get a raw deal, you just have to ________ it ________ you and carry on with your life.
5. In interviews, company CEOs often ________ ________ poor results and focus on the future.

About you

C Answer the questions with information that is true for you.

1. Do you know anyone who is easily talked into things? Explain.

____

____

2. Some difficult situations are easier to put behind you than others. Give your opinion.

____

____

3. Think of an example where a lot of people were taken in by someone or something.

____

____

Lesson B **Grammar** Referring to people and things

A Complete the article on identity theft with appropriate pronouns. Sometimes there is more than one correct answer.

Identity theft on social networking sites

We like to keep in touch with ________[1] on social networking sites, but are we protecting ________[2] against the dangers of identity theft? An online "poser" could be using your photos and other information to set up a fake profile and then presenting ________[3] or ________[4] to others as you. In such a situation, "you" may unwittingly find ________[5] spreading stories over the Internet, which seem believable because they include plausible information about your friends.

It's been widely reported how posers take people in by setting up celebrity profiles. They and their excited, naive fans then share personal information with ________[6]. Unfortunately, if you find ________[7] in this compromised situation, you may discover that things like driver's licenses and even credit cards are being issued in your name.

Sometimes your social network ________[8] isn't secure enough. So how does one go about safeguarding ________[9] against posers? People create risks by posting photos that are downloadable, and by sharing sensitive details about ________[10], like their address and date of birth. To be on the safe side, make sure that your social networking profile can only be accessed by trusted friends.

B Complete the sentences with appropriate pronouns. Sometimes there is more than one correct answer.

1. I found my favorite actor on a social networking site and we "friended" ____________ .
2. I fooled ____________ into believing that he was the real actor and not a poser.
3. Certain things should have given him away, like when he described ____________ as shy and lonely.
4. We chatted with ____________ for a few months, and he talked me into sharing a lot of personal information.
5. Eventually my sister, who is one of my social networking contacts, became suspicious and decided to investigate him ____________ .
6. She had picked up on the fact that we found ____________ being contacted by people we don't often communicate with.
7. A trail of clues led to a poser representing ____________ or herself as me on a different social networking site.
8. The site deleted the profile, but in the end, it comes down to you ____________ being careful about sharing personal information.
9. The experience ____________ turned out to be a useful one. I've been able to tell a lot of people about it. Hopefully, they'll be more careful, too.

About you

C How can we protect ourselves against identity theft? Give your opinion and include pronouns from the lesson in your answer.

____

____

____

____

Lesson C Conversation strategies

A Complete the conversation. Write a or b.

Kasia Pete keeps getting turned down for a rental apartment. He says it's because homeowners disapprove of his long hair.

Becky He might be right. I mean, I *like* his hair, and he'd be a good tenant. But at the same time, ____[1].

a. his hair creates an impression, and this is a conservative town
b. he'd be very reliable

Kasia Maybe. But if you look at it from Pete's perspective, ____[2].

a. he should get his hair cut
b. it's not fair to be judged on your appearance

Becky Yes, but homeowners don't want to take risks. And by the same token, tenants should ____[3].

a. realize that the more conservative they look, the better their chances of securing an apartment
b. be able to wear scruffy clothes if they like

Kasia Well, I can see it from both sides. I accept that homeowners don't want to take risks. ____[4].

a. They're being unreasonable
b. But they could check his references to find out what kind of person he really is

B Complete the conversations. Write the letters a–d. There is one extra answer.

1. *A* My friend Sue's a really good server. She gets lots of tips.
   B ____. People like it when servers look nice.
2. *A* My manager says she wants us all to look very stylish. She says it's good for business.
   B ____ Not everybody has the money to buy expensive clothes.
3. *A* My boss asked me if I still felt motivated. She said she'd noticed I wasn't wearing any makeup.
   B ____ Your appearance doesn't reflect your performance.

a. She could have anticipated that, to put it simply.
b. Well, that's none of her business, to put it politely.
c. That's really asking a bit much of people, to put it mildly.
d. Well, to put it bluntly, it's because she always looks fabulous.

C Circle the correct options to complete the conversations. Sometimes both are correct.

1. *A* One of my colleagues got really mad today. She came to work wearing this long dress, and one of the guys made some silly joke about her wearing a nightgown. She didn't like it, **equally / to put it mildly**.
   B Oh dear. I guess **if you look at it from / by the same token** the guy's perspective, it was just a joke. But, **at the same time / equally**, he should know not to comment on a colleague's appearance like that. It's unprofessional **equally / to put it bluntly**.
2. *A* My friend disapproves of commercials that only have good-looking people in them, **but I can see it from both sides / by the same token**. Companies have a right to sell products in the way they feel is best, don't you think?
   B Yes, **by the same token / at the same time**, they should have a sense of social responsibility. To put it **mildly / bluntly** commercials do tend to encourage the shallow obsession with looks that so many people have today.

Lesson D **Reading** Gender stereotypes

A Prepare **Check (✔) the statements that you think are true. Then read the article. Which statements are true according to Dr. Eliot?**

- ☐ Girls are more social and emotional than boys.
- ☐ Boys are more aggressive than girls.
- ☐ Girls are less competitive than boys.
- ☐ Boys are more athletic than girls.
- ☐ Girls write better than boys.
- ☐ Boys are better at reading maps than girls.

BOYS and GIRLS: not as different as we thought

1 For decades, psychologists and researchers have been telling us the same old thing — boys and girls are fundamentally different. Their brains are different, their childhood development is different, their perceptions of the world around them are different. It's the old nature versus nurture debate, with many parents unmistakably believing that nature is the primary force in a child's development and that all parents can do is hang on for the ride.

2 But a new book by Lise Eliot, PhD, suggests that many of these differences are what we, the adults, make of them. She's done the equivalent of a meta-analysis on the research foundation for gender differences between boys and girls, and put into a consumer-digestible format. The results are summarized in her new book, *Pink Brain, Blue Brain*. As *Newsweek* summarized:

> 3 How we perceive children — sociable or remote, physically bold or reticent — shapes how we treat them and therefore what experiences we give them. Since life leaves footprints on the very structure and function of the brain, these various experiences produce sex differences in adult behavior and brains — the result not of innate and inborn nature but of nurture.

4 The gist of her findings is that many of the differences that parents believe are innate or nature-led are not. Motor skills? The same. Ability to have deep emotional feelings? The same. Aggressiveness? The same. Why do we observe such differences in little boys and girls? Because parents often unconsciously reinforce the gender stereotypes within their children:

5 "Oh, little Sally can't run as quickly as little Bobby."

6 "Oh, Mikey is always so aggressive; Angela is an angel in comparison!"

7 "Since little Eric doesn't seem to express many emotions, he must not be as emotional as little Hannah, who has an outburst at the drop of a hat!"

8 Our children become a self-fulfilling prophecy — they turn into the kids we, by and large, imagine them to be. Parents don't usually do this consciously, of course. It is the stereotyped roles hammered into us at an early age, reinforced by consumerism and toy makers and commercials, and our own mothers and fathers. Boys are athletic and competitive, while girls are less so, and more social and emotional. These are stereotypes we imprint on our children; they are not naturally this way.

9 There are *some* differences the research supports with robust data. Dr. Eliot found that girls write better and more easily than most boys, and that boys have a better sense of spatial navigation than girls (like in reading a map).

10 What Dr. Eliot is saying isn't really new. We've known for years that infant brains are extremely malleable. But she's put it into simple language and has done a good job summarizing the vast body of research to really help put all of that data into some context. Her argument that small differences at birth become amplified over time as we all work to reinforce the gender stereotypes resonates.

11 Children must learn to stray from their comfort zones, with parents helping them try new things and explore new ways of expressing themselves that perhaps don't feel natural at first, but will often come with time. Boys, for instance, should be encouraged and reinforced for being able to express their feelings. The book not only goes into what few differences really exist, but also explains what parents can do to help encourage their kids to go outside of their comfort zones.

SOURCE: Psych Central

B Paraphrase **Write the number of the paragraph next to each description.**

1. Parents have long felt that they have no influence over the forces of nature that control their children. _____
2. What parents have believed to be innate differences between boys and girls was found to be reinforced by stereotypes, not biological. _____
3. Children become a product of what is expected of them. _____
4. There are ways to help children become better at the things that aren't stereotypical to their respective gender. _____

C Check your understanding **Complete the sentences. Write a, b, or c.**

1. There is an old view that boys and girls are different because _____ .
   a. their biological make up is different
   b. their experiences are different
   c. parents treat them differently
2. According to Dr. Eliot, there is _____ adult gender behavior and the experiences we had as children.
   a. no connection between
   b. a direct link between
   c. a lack of understanding about
3. Eliot claims the reason boys and girls behave differently is because parents _____ stereotyped behavior in children.
   a. deliberately reinforce
   b. unintentionally emphasize
   c. reluctantly encourage
4. Eliot describes how ideas like male athleticism and emotional females are reinforced by _____ .
   a. children's toys
   b. advertising
   c. both
5. The idea that girls are better at writing and boys are better at reading maps is _____
   a. untrue
   b. backed up by research
   c. possible, but not proven
6. The writer of the article respects Dr. Eliot's ability to _____ gender research.
   a. draw new conclusions from
   b. question existing
   c. present
7. Dr. Eliot's book explains strategies that parents can utilize to help their children _____ .
   a. become better at sports
   b. become better writers
   c. try new things

D Understanding inference **Check (✓) the statements that are suggested in the article.**

1. ☐ The idea that all gender differences are natural is old-fashioned.
2. ☐ Boys and girls perceive the world differently.
3. ☐ Most parents accept that nurture is as important as nature in a child's development.
4. ☐ Dr. Eliot's book has been written in a way that ordinary people will be able to understand.
5. ☐ Our life experiences can cause men to think like women and vice versa.
6. ☐ We force gender stereotypes onto young people.
7. ☐ Women become more interested in consumerism than boys because of gender stereotyping.
8. ☐ The book gives a balanced view of how nature and nurture influence our development.
9. ☐ Boys and girls rarely find any common interests until they grow up.

About you

E React **Do you think the media and the choices we make as consumers reinforce gender stereotypes? Give reasons for your answer.**

____

____

Writing A statistical report

A Circle the correct options to complete the statistical report.

READING *for* PLEASURE among American youth

Reading for pleasure among children is a practice that can significantly boost reading test scores. According to research on American schoolchildren by the Data Resource Center for Child and Adolescent Health, . . .

- 16 percent of children do not read at all. There are twice **more / as many** boys **as / than** girls in this category.
- 44 percent of children read for at least 30 minutes a day, and 24 percent read for 30 minutes to an hour. Boys are just as likely to be in the first group **as / than** girls, but girls are more likely **as / than** boys to be in the second.
- 16 percent of children read for more than an hour a day. There are roughly 1.5 times **as / as many** girls **as / than** boys in this group.

It is widely believed that reading regularly to preschool children encourages them to develop reading habits. A survey by the Federal Interagency Forum in Child and Family Statistics on the likelihood of preschool children being read to reveals that:

- children from poor families are nearly 25 percent less likely to be read to **as / than** children from average income families.
- the chances of children with college-educated mothers being read to are more than twice **as high as / higher** in many cases **as / than** children whose mothers didn't complete high school.

Sources: Data Resource Center for Child & Adolescent Health and Centers for Disease Control & Prevention

B Complete the comparisons in the sentences with the information in parentheses.

1. More wealth often means better health. Children from average income families are _________ to be in good health _________ children from poor families. (1.5 times / likely)
2. There are more boys than girls with Attention Deficit Disorder (ADD). Boys are about _________ to have ADD _________ girls. (twice / likely)
3. Most children are active after school. There are _________ children participating in after-school activities _________ children who don't participate at all. (five times / many)
4. On average, children with single mothers are absent from school more often. In the past 12 months, children in single-mother families missed school _________________ children in two-parent families. (twice / times)

C Editing Correct the errors. There is one error in each sentence.

1. The incidence of respiratory allergies is twice more common in children with poor health.
2. Children in single-mother families are more likely to have learning disabilities and ADD children in two-parent families.
3. Uninsured children are more than four times likely to have unmet dental needs as children with private health insurance.
4. In families with an income of less than $35,000, the percentage of children with a learning disability is twice higher as children in families with an income of $100,000 or more.

D Write a report on a health or education issue for a social studies class. Use at least one statistic to support your argument.

Listening extra Time for a change

A What would you be willing to change if your partner requested it? Check (✓) the items. Add two more ideas of things you would or would not be willing to change.

☐ your appearance
☐ your job
☐ the way you spend your free time
☐ what you eat

____

____

B Listen to Jules and Caitlin's conversation about their friend Marty. Check (✓) the topics they talk about.

☐ online dating
☐ Marty's appearance
☐ being on vacation
☐ Marty's job
☐ exercise routines
☐ household chores
☐ roommates
☐ leaving home
☐ Marty's motorcycle

C Listen again. Are the sentences true or false? Write T or F.

1. The relationship between Marty and his girlfriend is going well. _____
2. Marty's girlfriend described herself accurately in her online profile. _____
3. Marty refused to change his hairstyle. _____
4. Marty used to work as a waiter, but now he works in a grocery store. _____
5. Marty has always done his own laundry. _____
6. Marty is still living with his parents. _____
7. Marty sold his motorcycle to please his girlfriend. _____
8. Both of Marty's friends are surprised at the effect Marty's girlfriend has had on him. _____

D Circle the correct options to complete the sentences.

1. Marty met his girlfriend **through a friend / on the Internet**.
2. Marty's girlfriend **is / isn't** into nature in a big way.
3. Marty is **more / less** organized than his girlfriend.
4. Marty **sometimes / never** makes dinner for himself and his girlfriend.
5. Marty's parents always dreaded him **moving back into / moving out of** their home.
6. Marty's girlfriend has changed him **slightly / completely**.

About you

E Write about some changes you have made to your lifestyle over the years. What influenced you to make them?

____

____

____

____

Now complete the *Unit 12 Progress chart* on page 101.

Progress charts

Unit 7 Progress chart

Mark the boxes to rate your progress. ☑ I can do it. ? I can do it, but have questions. ! I need to review it. I can . . .	To review, go back to these pages in the Student's Book.
☐ discuss relationships, marriage, and family life.	74
☐ talk about the best ways to meet people.	76
☐ use conditional sentences without *if* to hypothesize.	75
☐ use *wh-* clauses as subjects and objects.	77
☐ use at least 12 expressions with *and, or, but* (*give and take*).	76
☐ use expressions like *in the end* and *in a word* to summarize or finish my points.	78
☐ use *then* to draw a conclusion from something someone said.	79
☐ write a magazine article expressing number and amount with expressions like *a number / great deal of* etc.	82

Unit 8 Progress chart

Mark the boxes to rate your progress. ☑ I can do it. ? I can do it, but have questions. ! I need to review it. I can . . .	To review, go back to these pages in the Student's Book.
☐ discuss people and events in history.	84, 86
☐ discuss the importance of history and one's family history.	89
☐ use the perfect infinitive to refer to past time.	85
☐ use cleft sentences beginning with *It* to focus on certain nouns, phrases, and clauses.	87
☐ use at least 10 adjective antonyms (*lasting—temporary; superficial—profound*).	86
☐ use expressions like *Let's not go there* to avoid talking about a topic.	88
☐ respond with *that's what I'm saying* to focus on my viewpoint.	89
☐ say perfect infinitives.	141
☐ write a narrative essay and order events in the past in different ways.	92

Unit 9 Progress chart

Mark the boxes to rate your progress. ☑ I can do it. ? I can do it, but have questions. ! I need to review it. I can . . .	To review, go back to these pages in the Student's Book.
☐ discuss feats, challenges, and developments in engineering, and robots.	94, 100
☐ evaluate priorities in research and development.	99
☐ use *–ever* words to talk about unknown people or things.	95
☐ use negative adverbs (*never, not only*) + inversion to start a sentence.	97
☐ use at least 12 expressions to describe engineering projects (*erect, install*).	96
☐ use expressions like *given (that)* to introduce facts that support my opinions.	98
☐ emphasize negative phrases with *at all* and *whatsoever.*	99
☐ use fall-rise intonation for background information.	142
☐ write a classification essay; express alternatives using *rather than, as opposed to,* etc.	102

Unit 10 Progress chart

Mark the boxes to rate your progress. ☑ I can do it. ? I can do it, but have questions. ! I need to review it. I can . . .	To review, go back to these pages in the Student's Book.
☐ discuss the news, how it is reported, and if speed or accuracy is more important.	106, 111
☐ evaluate how much you trust what you hear or read in the news.	112
☐ use continuous infinitive forms to report events in progress.	107
☐ use the subjunctive to describe what should happen, what is important, and to refer to demands and recommendations.	109
☐ use at least 10 collocations with verbs and nouns (*undergo surgery*).	106
☐ highlight topics by putting them at the start or end of what I say.	110
☐ use *this* and *these* or *that* and *those* in conversation.	111
☐ use stress and intonation in longer sentences.	142
☐ summarize an article; choose singular or plural verbs.	114

Unit 11 Progress chart

Mark the boxes to rate your progress. ☑ I can do it. ? I can do it, but have questions. ! I need to review it. I can . . .	To review, go back to these pages in the Student's Book.
☐ discuss what is real and what isn't.	116, 121
☐ discuss how you would handle an emergency.	117
☐ use *be to* expressions to talk about the future.	117
☐ use passive verb complements.	119
☐ use 10 idioms with *turn* (*turn over a new leaf, turn around*).	118
☐ use expressions like *That's my concern* to express concerns.	120
☐ use *to me* to introduce an opinion.	121
☐ use stress in longer idioms.	143
☐ write an essay using academic conjunctions and expressions (*provided that, regardless of*).	124

Unit 12 Progress chart

Mark the boxes to rate your progress. ☑ I can do it. ? I can do it, but have questions. ! I need to review it. I can . . .	To review, go back to these pages in the Student's Book.
☐ discuss independence, the psychology of attraction, the brain, and stereotypes.	126, 131
☐ discuss the differences between online and in-person relationships.	128
☐ use objects + *-ing* forms after prepositions and verbs.	127
☐ use reflexive pronouns and *one another, each other.*	129
☐ use 10 new phrasal verbs (*go by, pick up on*).	128
☐ use expressions to consider different points of view and give information.	130
☐ use *to put it bluntly, mildly* etc. to indicate how I choose to express my opinions.	131
☐ use stress with reflexive pronouns.	143
☐ write a report using statistics; use expressions like *twice as likely, four times more often.*	134

Author acknowledgements

The authors would like to thank everyone who contributed material and ideas to this workbook: Guy de Villiers, Deborah Gordon, Natasha Isadora, Therese Naber, Allison Ramage, and Mary Vaughn.

Photography credits

50 Derek Latta/iStockphoto **51** Exactostock/SuperStock **52** Oksancia/Shutterstock **53** ChinaFotoPres/Getty Images **54** *(top to bottom)* Stockbroker/SuperStock; Catherine Yeulet/iStockphoto; *(background)* siamionau pavel/ Shutterstock **56** ciarada/Shutterstock **57** Blend Images/SuperStock **58** Getty Images **59** *(top to bottom)* Evans/ Three Lions/Getty Images; Roger Viollet/Getty Images; *(background)* MaxyM/Shutterstock **60** *(clockwise from top left)* Image Asset Management Ltd./SuperStock; Christie's Images Ltd./SuperStock; Image Asset Management Ltd./SuperStock **61** Exactostock/SuperStock **62** *(top)* Duncan Walker/iStockphoto; (bottom) farbled/Shutterstock; *(background)* farbled/Shutterstock **64** *(top to bottom)* absolut/Shutterstock; Daily Herald Archive/SSPL **65** appleuzr/iStockphoto **67** Robert Maass/CORBIS **68** *(top to bottom)* Photononstop/ SuperStock; © MAPS.com/CORBIS **70** Michael Rosenfeld/Maximilian S/SuperStock **72** *(top to bottom)* Photononstop/SuperStock; YONHAP/epa/Corbis **74** GrandeDuc/Shutterstock **75** Cusp/SuperStock **76** Menna/ Shutterstock **78** Ice-Storm/Shutterstock **79** macgyverhh/Shutterstock **82** pio3/Shutterstock **83** Thinkstock **86** AFP/Getty Images **88** Christophe Cerisier/iStockphoto **91** Richard Levine/Alamy **92** Cienpies Design/ Shutterstock **93** Thinkstock/RF **94** *(top to bottom)* Zurijeta/Shutterstock; Ignite Lab/Shutterstock **96** Jason Stitt/Shutterstock **97** Giorgio Magini/iStockphoto

Text credits

The authors and publishers are grateful for permission to reprint the following items:

54 "The Importance of Family Dinners" from edis.ifas.ufl.edu/fy1054. Reprinted by permission. **62** "Going to California - 49ers and the Gold Rush" from americanhistory.about.com/library/weekly/aa090901a.htm. Reprinted by permission. **70** "Robots are taking mid-level jobs, changing the economy" by Sharon Gaudin on www. computerworld.com, October 31, 2011. Reprinted by permission. **78** "Why Are Newspapers Dying?" from journalism.about.com/od/trends/a/dyingpapers.htm. Reprinted by permission. **86** "Second Mona Lisa unveiled for first time in 40 years" from www.abcnews.go.com/blogs/headlines/2012/09/second-mona-lisa-unveiled-for-first-time-in-40-years. Reprinted by permission. **94** "Boys and Girls: Not As Different As We Thought" from psychcentral.com/blog/archives/2009/09/05/boys-and-girls-not-as-different-as-we-thought. Reprinted by permission.

Every effort has been made to trace the owners of copyrighted material in this book. We would be grateful to hear from anyone who recognizes his or her copyrighted material and who is unacknowledged. We will be pleased to make the necessary corrections in future editions of the book.

Corpus

Development of this publication has made use of the Cambridge English Corpus (CEC). The CEC is a computer database of contemporary spoken and written English, which currently stands at over one billion words. It includes British English, American English and other varieties of English. It also includes the Cambridge Learner Corpus, developed in collaboration with the University of Cambridge ESOL Examinations. Cambridge University Press has built up the CEC to provide evidence about language use that helps to produce better language teaching materials.